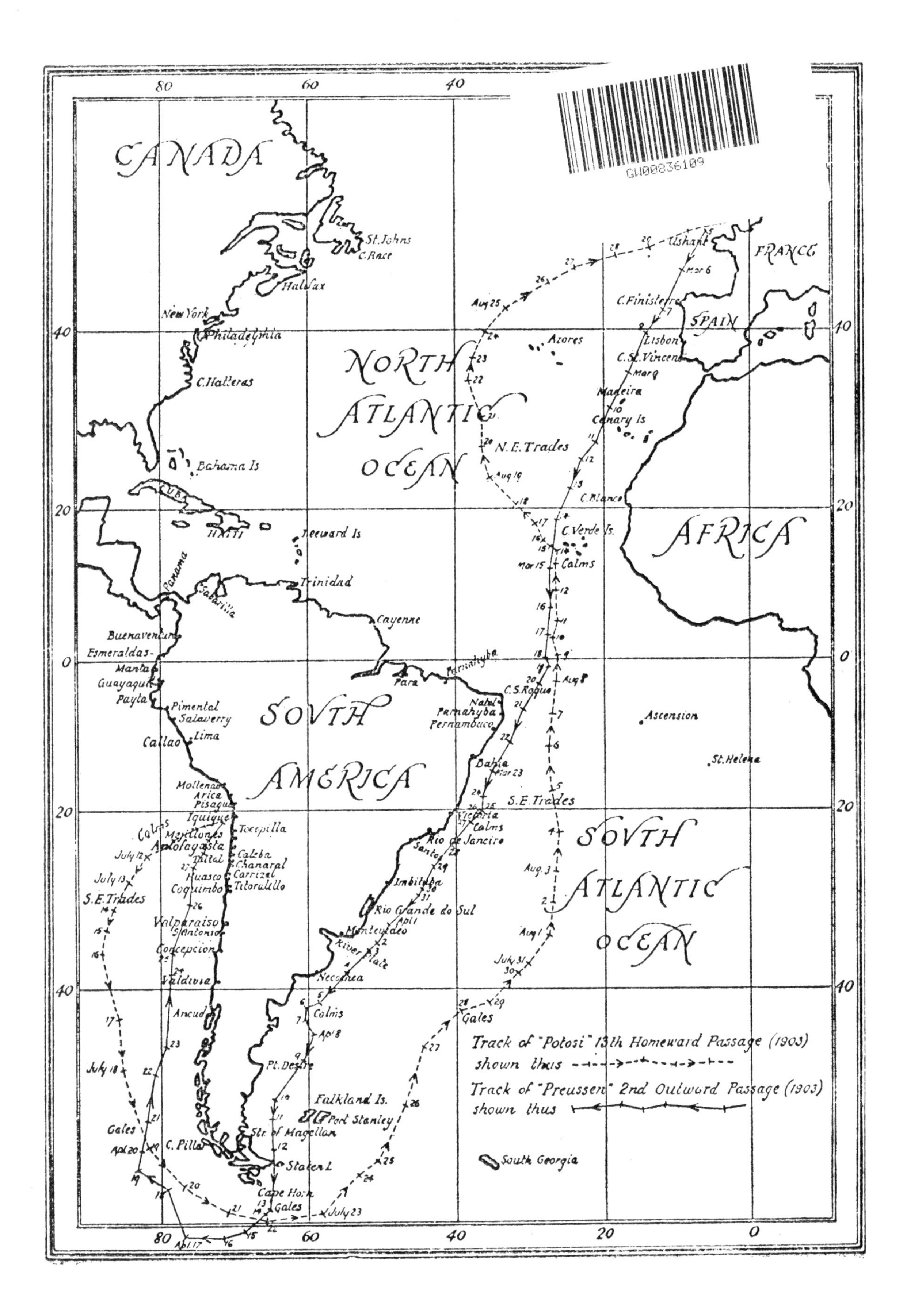
CANADA
NORTH ATLANTIC OCEAN
SOUTH AMERICA
SOUTH ATLANTIC OCEAN
AFRICA
FRANCE
SPAIN
St. Johns
C. Race
Halifax
New York
Philadelphia
C. Hatteras
Bahama Is
Leeward Is
Trinidad
Cayenne
Para
Natal
Pernambuco
Bahia
Rio de Janeiro
Rio Grande do Sul
Montevideo
River Plate
Falkland Is.
Port Stanley
Str. of Magellan
Staten I.
Cape Horn
South Georgia
Ushant
C. Finisterre
Lisbon
C. St. Vincent
Azores
Madeira
Canary Is
C. Blanco
C. Verde Is.
Ascension
St. Helena
N. E. Trades
S. E. Trades
Calms
Gales
Buenaventura
Esmeraldas
Manta
Guayaquil
Payta
Pimental
Salaverry
Callao
Lima
Mollendo
Arica
Pisagua
Iquique
Tocopilla
Antofagasta
Taltal
Caleta
Chanaral
Carrizal
Huasco
Coquimbo
Valparaiso
S. Antonio
Concepcion
Valdivia
Ancud
Pt. Desire
C. Pillar
Track of "Potosi" 13th Homeward Passage (1903) shown thus
Track of "Preussen" 2nd Outward Passage (1903) shown thus

The Nitrate Clippers

BY THE SAME AUTHOR

The China Clippers
The Colonial Clippers
The Blackwall Frigates
The Log of the "Cutty Sark"
The Western Ocean Packets
The Last of the Windjammers, Vol. I.
The Last of the Windjammers, Vol. II.
The Down Easters
The Opium Clippers
The Arctic Whalers
The Coolie Ships and Oil Sailers

"PADUA"

From a Drawing by E. W. Petrejus [*Frontispiece.*

THE NITRATE CLIPPERS

BY

BASIL LUBBOCK

WITH ILLUSTRATIONS

GLASGOW
BROWN, SON & FERGUSON, LTD., NAUTICAL PUBLISHERS
52 DARNLEY STREET

New Edition 1932
Reprinted - 1976

ISBN 0 85174 116 9

Printed and Made in Great Britain

Dedicated to

All Old West Coasters

PREFACE

LIKE most Englishmen I have been brought up in the belief that as sailormen we are without rivals and that our ships are better designed, better built and better sailed than those of any other nation.

This superiority complex, which must often have proved somewhat irritating to other great seafaring nations, is fast being dissipated in these days.

Indeed, I fear that at the present time we have little right to claim superiority either in seamanship, maritime science or ship construction over nations which our seafaring grandfathers were wont to allude to somewhat rudely as Dutchmen and Dagoes.

At one time, it is true, we seemed to be leading the field, to use a racing parlance, but can we truthfully say that to-day? I doubt it.

Those who fear comparisons maintain that they are odious, but healthy rivalry is the only way in which man, with his lazy nature and slack brain, can be kept up to the mark.

In the Mercantile Marine, in the Fishing Industry, aye, and in the Royal Navy itself we have still much that needs improvement, and there is much that we can learn from other seafaring nations.

In this book I have given a slight history of the famous nitrate ships of F. Laeisz and A. D. Bordes, and I owe much of my information to the kindness of these two great shipping firms. I also have to thank many friends in England and Chile for invaluable help.

PREFACE

I have been lucky in obtaining some rare photographs as illustrations, which I know will be appreciated by all sailing ship lovers.

My readers will, I feel sure, agree that these "P" Line and A. D. Bordes' nitrate ships deserve to be remembered in the history of the sea along with our own clippers and carriers, for finer, better run ships could not have been found in our British Sailing Marine, even at the height of its glory.

NOTE.—The "mile" in this book refers to the sea mile of 6080 feet and not the statute or land mile of 5280 feet.

NOTE.— The war referred to in this book, unless otherwise stated, is that of 1914-18.

CONTENTS

PART I.—THE WEST COAST.

PART II.—THE CLIPPERS.

CONTENTS

APPENDIX

ILLUSTRATIONS

ILLUSTRATIONS

THE NITRATE CLIPPERS

PART I.—THE WEST COAST.

Stretching due South the Equator
  Swept by a mountainous swell.
Mixture of pampa and jungle,
  Where gringoes and centipedes dwell,
Cursed by all manners of fevers,
  Hotter and drier than Hell
        Is the Coast.

Seaports where life is a burden
  Menaced by typhoid and stinks,
Home of the "down-and-the-outer,"
  Of dreary beachcombers and "ginks,"
Where the only diversions for gringoes
  Are loving, and gambling and drinks
        On the Coast.

Days when the mercury rises
  To ninety-and-nine in the shade,
Ev'nings when landscape and ocean,
  In crimson and gold are arrayed,
Nights when the heavenly ceiling
  With glittering stardust's inlaid
        On the Coast.

From *The Coast.* By R. H. AITKIN.

The Glamour of the West Coast of South America.

OST of the present day seamen who were trained in sail have memories of the W.C.S.A., both pleasant and unpleasant, tragic and even comic. The West Coast, with its steep, treeless hills simmering in the heat, ankle deep in dust, and swarming with flies; with its smelly dobe and mortar shacks in narrow twisting streets; and its heaving windless anchorages, possesses a glamour which is all its own.

To the newcomer the coast from Guayaquil to Coronel seems entirely dreary and God-forsaken—a coast where men walked in fear, and the women, behind their bars, listened unconsciously for the dreaded "terremoto." In the old days it used to be the refuge of worn-out ships and men who preferred the beach to the brace, and the easy, lax ways of the tropics to the strenuous life-struggle in the temperate zones.

Many a sailor, too, succumbed to the insidious attraction of the West Coast; and, after deserting from his ship, settled down in Iquique or Callao as a pisco vendor, a boarding-house master, or the proprietor of a fandango hall—that is to say if he had the strength of mind and energy to resist the attractions of beachcombing.

The inhabitants of the West Coast can be listed under the following headings: the Chileno or Peruvian aristocrat with his haughty Spanish blood and grand manner, the Indian drudge, and the ubiquitous half-caste. To these must be added the gringo and the beachcomber, offshoots and outcasts from the business of the sea.

The Navies of Chile and Peru were mostly manned by deserters from European and American ships. These wild reckless tars were the chief mainstay in a fight, but the terror of the vigilantes when busting their dollars ashore. Their pay, however, was generally, overdue and rarely forthcoming until the black-eyed Dolores and shrill-voiced Juanita from Maintop Hill, Valpo, had issued an ultimatum to the paymaster. Then, when the leave boats pulled ashore, it must be confessed that the senoritas, with their flashing glances and gleaming teeth, had a hard task in pitting their charms against those of the fiery anisardo, aquardiente, and pisco, which, at a chaouch

(20 cents) a bottle, was an attraction such as few old-time sailors could resist. Leave days on the West Coast generally ended in the calaboose. It would be hard to say how many penniless gringoes have landed on the mole at Valparaiso; or the number of shipless seamen who have camped on the bales round the Custom-house at Iquique.

One night the threadbare gang on the "gunnies" included a Pat who was something of a poet, and he treated his mates to the following song:

> I stood on the bales at midnight
> As the "plaza" clock struck the hour,
> And the moon rose o'er Iquique
> Behind the Custom's tower.
>
> As I heard the waters breaking
> Against the landing pier,
> A flood of thoughts came o'er me
> And nearly brought a tear.
>
> How often, oh! how often,
> In the days that had gone by
> I had hid midst the bales at midnight
> And heard the police pass by.
>
> How often, oh! how often,
> In the days that had gone by,
> I had lain on the bales at twilight
> And seen old Jimmy go by.
>
> How often, oh! how often,
> I had wished that a tidal wave
> Would bear him away on its bosom,
> And find him a watery grave.
>
> For my tongue was dry and restless
> And my pocket full of care,
> And the burden on my liver
> Seem'd greater than it could bear,

But hospitable Iquique
On the bales gives lodging free,
And only my loss to skippers
Throws its shadow over me.

Yet whenever I cross the "plaza"
And see the captains there,
I remember, begorrah! the ocean,
My home for many a year.

Ashore for ever? Nay, never,
So long as this life does last,
So long as this heart has passions
I must go before the mast.

But Harvey with his broken finger,
"Happy Jack" with his classical nose,
Neither's the friend of the singer
Who's just related his woes.

The names mentioned in this doggerel were those of seamen's boarding-house masters. It used to be said at one time that the West Coast was noted for its unscrupulous boarding-house masters, its beachcombers, and its horse mackerel.

It is only within the last 150 years that man has invaded the W.C.S.A. in any numbers. Except for a few poor Indians, the West Coast and its seas used to be entirely the domain of the fin and feather tribes. Even at the present day in many a quiet cove, where the water is as transparent as glass, one cannot see the bottom for fish; whilst overhead millions of gulls, terns, petrels, and pelicans, not to mention guano birds, fly in such vast flocks as to darken the sun.

Trade on the Coast.

The first ships on the Coast were the treasure galleons of the Spaniards, who, after enslaving the Indians and putting them to work in the silver mines, loaded the plate into these lumbering vessels and transported it across to the Philippines.

These were the galleons which Drake, Woodes Rogers, Shelvocke and Anson preyed upon. Then about a hundred years after Anson the stout little Welsh copper ore barques appeared on the Coast. Close on their heels came the guano ships. Finally, the West Coast became the loading station of the superb nitrate clipper.

The copper ore used to be brought from the interior on the backs of llamas. The guano was dug from the Chinchas and other islands, whilst the nitrate was mined in the great salt desert of Tarapaca, whence it was conveyed in the early days by pack mules and donkeys. These poor animals had a very short life owing to want of food and water, for all the water had to be condensed and there was no herbage on the trails to the Coast. Of late years the nitrate has all been conveyed by rail, except in certain places where it can be loaded into cars which run down on a mono-rail by means of a wire cable leading from the heights to the lighters.

Neither copper ore, guano nor nitrate were ideal cargoes, and until quite recent years they were considered to be only fit for second-class ships. Since the early nineties, however, all three commodities have become very necessary to the civilised world and the trades are no longer looked down upon.

The guano islands mostly consist of volcanic rock, which is covered by guano to the depth of from 50 to as much as 200 feet. The yellow guano dust blows in clouds from the workings and covers everything in its path. Only fleas and lizards are indifferent to its ammoniacal properties. The smartest ship when loading guano became covered from truck to water-line in the dust. But it was easily washed off, and a vessel, when her hatches were clapped on, could soon be restored to her original spick and span condition.

As regards nitrate, this chemical has many peculiar properties. It is very deliquescent and quickly soluble in water. It has to be well dunnaged and stowed dry, and when it is very green there is a good deal of shrinkage. The evaporation from nitrate kills rats, mice, and all other vermin, even to wood lice. Cats also are affected by nitrate cargo. Very often they take to lying on the nitrate, become very lethargic, and will not leave the spot. Finally they get weaker and weaker until they crawl away and die.

As a cargo nitrate makes a ship very stiff. The greatest danger attached to it is the danger of fire. The only way that nitrate can be put out once it has caught fire is by means of water which has had nitrate soaking in it. This nitrate-water was kept ready in barrels alongside each hatch whilst nitrate was being loaded. Nevertheless, many a fine ship was burnt whilst she was taking on her cargo. The instances which immediately spring to my mind are the ***Ross-shire***, ***Reliance***, and ***Duns Law***, all three of which were completely burnt out.

Cheering the Homeward Bounder.

In the good old days when the world was not so crowded, the sailing of a ship was recognised as an event which was too important to go unnoticed, and thus various ceremonies became usual at the distant ports of the world to celebrate the departure of the homeward bounder.

Usually these ceremonies took the simple form of shooting off guns, firing rockets and cheering. Thus, when a tea clipper sailed from Foochow or Shanghai every ship in the anchorage fired a salvo of its guns, which, in the case of the old Indiamen, extended the length of the main deck, but in the tea clippers only consisted of a couple of brass signalling guns. The wads of these saluting popguns were often rammed in very tight and hard in order to increase the loudness of the report, and if one of these hardened wads chanced to hit anything it did considerable damage. More than once it happened that a passing junk received a wad through its sail, making a hole as large as that of a 5·9 shell. But the Chinaman had to put up with the damage, for in those days the ruling races were accustomed to treat those who were not their equals in strength without much consideration, and a damaged sail, or even a damaged Chinee, was all part of the fun when the Anglo-Saxon seaman was celebrating.

In no part of the world was the ceremony of cheering the homeward bounder so elaborate as on the West Coast, and it has only died with the disappearance of sail. In August, 1927, the British ship *William Mitchell* loaded nitrate at Tocopilla. Her officers were old West Coasters, and the ceremony of cheering the last bag was performed with all the usual trimmings; but the only vessels in port with her were steamers, and not a single one of them took the least notice or attempted to play their part in the time-honoured ceremony.

The ceremony of cheering the last bag of cargo as it came aboard was followed the same night by that of cheering the homeward bounder. Most of the ships coming to the West Coast in the last days of sail brought coal, either from Europe or Australia, and it even became usual to cheer the last basket of coal as it went out of the ship as well as the last bag of saltpetre coming in.

The usual custom when cheering the last bag was as follows: As the bag was hoisted over the rail the youngest member of the crew, who was usually the smallest apprentice, jumped on to it with the national flag of his ship in his hand. He was then raised high enough for all the ships around to see, and proceeded to shout out at the top of his voice, "Three cheers for the captain, officers, and crew of —— " (the name of his ship). Then he was lowered and hoisted again three times, whilst he wildly waved the flag, and before he and the bag were lowered through the hatch he called for "Three cheers for all the ships in the harbour," which was responded to in stentorian tones.

That night at 8 p.m. the homeward bounder started to ring her bell. Immediately every ship followed suit until all the poop and foc's'le bells in port were ringing wildly. The tones of the bells echoed amongst the hills and valleys ashore, and were often audible for miles out to sea. This racket continued for ten or fifteen minutes, and whilst it was going on the homeward bounder proceeded to hoist a wooden framework aloft on the foremast, on which lighted riding lights were lashed in the form of the constellation of the Southern Cross.

A smart ship would go further than this by adding a long swinging outrigger which held two more lights, these being supposed to represent the Twin Centaurs. At the same time a captain who was not afraid of a little expense, and was jealous of his ship's reputation, would outline his rail and even his masts with coloured lights. The crew, too, of the homeward bounder would crowd on to the top of the midship-house and the foc's'le-head, each man holding a lighted torch of saltpetre. Some ships did not hoist the Southern Cross until the bell ringing had stopped, then sent it up to the strains of a favourite shanty, which, breaking out into the tropic night in the sudden deep hush which followed the din of the bells, was often

IQUIQUE (ABOUT 1893-5)

Lent by Nautical Photo Agency   Fred C. Poyser.

See page 4

"PAMIR" IN BALLAST OFF SAN ANTONIO

[*See page* 100

extremely impressive, especially when well sung by a good deep-water crew.

As soon as the Southern Cross had been hoisted the ceremony of cheering began. The man with the mightiest voice on the homeward bound ship sang out "Three cheers for the *Pitlochry*" (we will imagine that this is the name of the nearest vessel). Immediately these cheers had been given the *Pitlochry* replied with "Three cheers for the homeward bounder!" It is noticeable here that the etiquette of the ceremony demanded that the name of the homeward bounder should not be given. That was only said when cheering the last bag, but in the evening performance the cheers were always given for "the homeward bounder." The ceremony then went on until every ship in port had been cheered and had given her cheers for the homeward bounder.

At some ports it was the custom to ring the ship's bell before each round of cheers. The din may be imagined, when, as often happened in one of the big nitrate ports, there were fifty or sixty ships in port and possibly two or three homeward bounders on the same night. When two homeward bounders were cheering each other, each tried to outdo the other in the various noises she could produce.

As soon as the last cheers had died down the captain of the homeward bound vessel had a further opportunity of doing his ship proud. Some homeward bounders then proceeded to give a very fine firework display, with rockets, Roman candles, etc. It was also the custom for her to send a boat round the nearest ships, and especially to her chum ships, with a bottle of grog aboard for each.

By 10 o'clock, as a rule, the fireworks had ceased, and the

anchorage had quieted down except for spasmodic outbursts of song or cheering. By this time the homeward bounder was surrounded by a flotilla of boats, for her skipper was entertaining all the captains in port and their ladies, as well as many of the shipping people from the shore. Her half-deck, too, was flowing over with apprentices, most of whom had rowed their captains aboard, but many besides were there on leave or without leave bidding good-bye to their chums.

Last of all, before all hands turned in, and as soon as the Southern Cross and other lights had been lowered down, everybody aboard the homeward bounder joined in singing the "Homeward Bound" shanty.

> O fare you well, I wish you well!
> Good-bye, fare you well; good-bye, fare you well!
> O, fare you well, my bonny young girls!
> Hoorah, my boys, we're homeward bound!

The Dangers and Difficulties of the West Coast Navigation.

Although steamers have no difficulties in navigating up and down the W.C.S.A. it is far otherwise with sailing ships. Although the passage North along the coast is assisted by wind and current, the passage South is a very different matter, and vessels which made the coast to the northward, and therefore to leeward, of their port often doubled the length of their passage. For instance, in 1903 the *Lindisfarne*, bound for Antofagasta from Australia, drifted to the North of her port in the grip of the current, and was compelled to sail Sou'west for 1300 miles and follow the usual track up the coast again in order to fetch Antofagasta. From the time when she drifted past Antofagasta to that when she made the port again from the southward was just one month.

In 1908 the *Hougomont* left Coquimbo for Tocopilla. She also failed to make the anchorage, and, drifting past it, was carried 400 miles to the northward, whereupon her captain threw up his charter in disgust and sailed away for Australia.

The *Buteshire* in 1909 left Panama for Caleta Coloso, and after struggling to get South for 80 days was compelled to put back to Panama, where she arrived after a fruitless passage of 91 days. This vessel was specially unlucky, for she then received orders to sail North to Portland, Oregon. A hundred and twenty-three days later she turned up at Acapulco, having averaged less than 10 miles a day. After this second failure she also left the coast for Australia.

Sailing ships have not only drifted past their port on the West Coast, but have drifted ashore. Such a fate happened to the *Algoa Bay* on January 24, 1905, when bound from Callao to San Fernando Island in ballast. She drifted ashore in St. Nicholas Bay. Three years later, on March 30, 1908, the *St. Mary's Bay* had a like fate, drifting ashore near Taltal when bound from Newcastle, N.S.W., to that port.

The *Nivelle* was lost on June 29, 1906, when she drifted into the breakers at Port Rincon, the water being too deep to anchor. Luckily for her crew, her master, realising his plight, acted with great promptitude, and got all hands into the boats clear of the ship in time. Both he and the mate were commended at the Inquiry, the chief cause of the loss being attributed to a faulty chronometer.

One could go on giving instances of this sort at the rate of one and two a year for over 50 years.

It is a question whether there have been more wrecks on the island of Mocha or on that of Santa Maria. Mocha is spoken of as a veritable ships' sepulchre. It has an interesting history could it only be written. In 1535 Magellan landed on Mocha Island, and surrounding the Indians on the hill called El Morro de los Chinos, he slaughtered a great number of them, as is proved by the quantity of skulls which have been dug up from time to time.

Drake also had a fight with the Indians on this island, during which, so tradition goes, he lost two or three of his front teeth.

Occasionally pieces of silver plate are washed up on the shore to the eastward of the Administrator's house. These are said to have come from the wreck of a Spanish galleon.

Of more modern ships wrecked on the island the total count cannot be ascertained, but here are the names of a few: *Race Horse*, owned by Paddy Conlin, a retired P.S.N.Co. skipper, went ashore at the North end of the island during a norther. Her figure-head is still to be seen in the Administrator's garden. Other names are those of the *Rosita*, a copper ore barque, and the *Downiemount*, also a barque, whose bones, I believe, are still to be seen.

Of steamers wrecked in the neighbourhood the best known are the *Illimani* and the *Valdivia*.

The last sailing ship to be wrecked on Santa Maria Island was the notorious *Garthwray*.

Another vessel which fell a victim to Santa Maria was the *Talavera*, one of the fastest and most beautiful little four-mast barques ever built. She stranded on the North-east end of the island on May 2, 1896.

Earthquakes and Tidal Waves.

Although the shipmaster sometimes had an anxious time in his traverses on the W.C.S.A., his ship was very often exposed to greater danger when at anchor than when she was under way, for she was liable to be overwhelmed by the furious norther or the still more terrible tidal wave. Few parts of the world have had such an awful experience of tidal waves as the West Coast of South America. Both inland and on the coast the chief towns of Chile and Peru have been destroyed again and again by earthquakes, the destruction and loss of life at the ports being made still more complete by tremendous tidal waves, which swept large ships right over the flattened houses.

Perhaps some account of these tidal waves may be of interest. On March 4, 1835, the *Beagle*, commanded by Captain Fitzroy, and with the famous Charles Darwin on board, beat up to the anchorage off Talcahuano just 12 days after that port and the town of Concepcion had been destroyed by an earthquake and tidal wave. Darwin at once seized the opportunity to gain first-hand evidence regarding these terrible convulsions of nature, and his account of this earthquake is of very great interest. To seamen his details of the tidal wave are of special value, and I will therefore quote from *A Naturalist's Voyage Round the World.*

Apparently the first signs of the earthquake were two large explosions seen out in the Bay, one of which appeared like a column of smoke, and the other like the blowing of a great whale.

The water also appeared everywhere to be boiling; it became black, and exhaled the most disagreeable sulphurous smell. Shortly after the shock a great wave was seen from the distance of three or four miles, approaching in the middle of the bay with a smooth outline; but along the shore it tore up cottages and trees as it swept onwards with irresistible force. At the head of the bay it broke in a fearful line of white breakers, which rushed up to a height of 23 vertical feet above the highest spring tides. Their force must have been prodigious; for at the Fort a cannon with its carriage, estimated at 4 tons in weight, was moved 15 feet inwards. A schooner was left in the midst of the ruins, 200 yards from the beach.

The first wave was followed by two others, which in their retreat carried away a vast wreck of floating objects. In one part of the bay a ship was pitched high and dry on shore, was carried off, again driven on shore, and again carried off. In another part two large vessels anchored near together were whirled about, and their cables were thrice wound round each other: though anchored at a depth of 36 feet they were for some minutes aground.

The great wave must have travelled slowly, for the inhabitants of Talcahuano had time to run up the hills behind the town; and some sailors pulled out seaward, trusting successfully to their boat riding securely over the swell, if they could reach it before it broke. One old woman with a little boy, four or five years old, ran into a boat, but there was nobody to row it out: the boat was consequently dashed against an anchor and cut in twain; the old woman was drowned, but the child was picked up some hours afterwards clinging to the wreck.

According to Darwin, the land round Concepcion Bay was raised from 2 to 3 feet in the great earthquake of 1835. The island of Santa Maria also, which is 30 miles from Concepcion, had sea shells clinging to rocks which were 10 feet above high water. These raisings of the land very often slowly subsided again after a few months.

Since 1835 the following seem to have been the worst of the West Coast quakes and waves.

The famous port of Iquique was almost destroyed by an earthquake in 1866, and also in 1877, on which occasion the town was overwhelmed by earthquakes, fire and tidal waves.

Valparaiso has suffered from earthquakes in 1730, 1822, 1839, 1873, and 1906; but that port seems to have been spared the terrible tidal waves. In 1873 there used to be three very disreputable drinking and dancing saloons on the edge of the cliffs above the harbour. These were called the Fore, Main, and Mizen Tops, and the earthquake of 1873 seemed to be designed specially for their destruction, for at the second quake all three were tumbled into the bay, along with their rascally proprietors, drink-sodden fiddlers, painted dancing girls, and their sailor-drugging crimps and runners.

Perhaps the worse port to suffer from tidal waves has been Arica, which has been three times destroyed since 1832. Arica was the centre of the earthquake of August 13, 1868, when the seaports from Iquique to Callao were swept by the waves, and Arequipa, 60 miles inland, was laid in ruins.

There are three definite stages in a West Coast earthquake. The first is called the "tremblor," a slight but rapid vibration occurring at frequent intervals. Then comes the "terremoto," a violent horizontal or rotary quake which is caused by the fracture of the earth's strata. This "terremoto," which may be repeated several times, is usually too fierce for any building to withstand. Finally the tidal wave arrives to complete the destruction and drown those wretched people who have been caught in the ruins of their houses.

During the August convulsion at Arica the town was laid in ruins by the "terremoto" at 5 p.m. Half an hour later the lower part was submerged by a tidal wave. This wave, which was not a very high one and did not break, then receded, and the shipping in the bay, which before the earthquake had been lying in 8 fathoms, actually grounded on their anchors. Then a second tidal wave came along, and this one was far more terrible than the first, for it was 60 feet high and breaking. It took the Peruvian frigate *Americana* and threw her 300 yards above high water mark, most of her officers and 130 of her crew being drowned. The Liverpool barque *Chanarcillo* was thrown 500 yards above high water mark. Captain Fox of this barque happened to be ashore when the quake occurred, and he immediately sent off his boat to bring all hands ashore to help the panic-stricken inhabitants of Arica, but those who were left behind on the vessel were all drowned.

The following vessels were also destroyed with all hands: The American store ship *Fredonia*; the Peruvian barque *Rosa Riviera*, and the brig *Edoardo.*

The scene amidst the ruins of Arica before the second tidal wave arrived was most heartrending. Many of the inhabitants were buried up to their necks, and everywhere shrieks of agony and cries of lamentation were to be heard. Then, when the second wave broke over the city, all human voices were drowned, and only the roar of the water and a terrible rumbling could be heard.

There is no doubt that a big earthquake affects the whole West Coast line of America from Concepcion Bay in the South to San Francisco Bay in the North. The terrible August earthquake of 1868 on the South Coast was followed by almost as severe a quake at San Francisco a month later, on September 21, when most of the chief buildings of the city came down and the earth opened in great cracks, through which the sea spouted up. And the Valparaiso earthquake of August 13, 1906, followed the great San Francisco cataclysm of April 18, 1906.

Mr. Frederick Perry, in the last chapter of his book, *Fair Winds and Foul,* has given a most dramatic account of the tidal wave which suddenly overwhelmed the little Peruvian

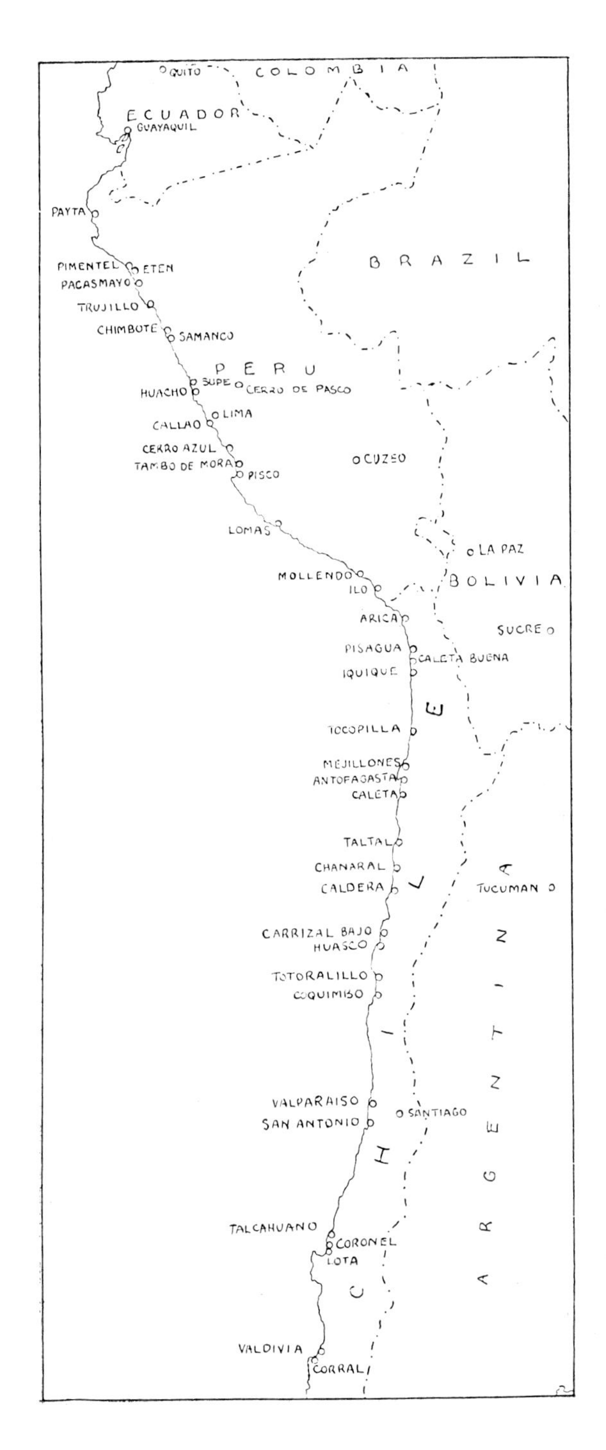
QUITO
COLOMBIA
ECUADOR
GUAYAQUIL
PAYTA
BRAZIL
PIMENTEL
ETEN
PACASMAYO
TRUJILLO
CHIMBOTE
SAMANCO
PERU
SUPE
HUACHO
CERRO DE PASCO
LIMA
CALLAO
CERRO AZUL
TAMBO DE MORA
PISCO
CUZCO
LOMAS
LA PAZ
MOLLENDO
BOLIVIA
ILO
ARICA
SUCRE
PISAGUA
CALETA BUENA
IQUIQUE
TOCOPILLA
MEJILLONES
ANTOFAGASTA
CALETA
TALTAL
CHANARAL
CALDERA
TUCUMAN
CARRIZAL BAJO
HUASCO
TOTORALILLO
COQUIMBO
VALPARAISO
SAN ANTONIO
SANTIAGO
TALCAHUANO
CORONEL
LOTA
VALDIVIA
CORRAL
CHILE
ARGENTINA

[*See page* **13**

"AVONMORE"

Lent by James Randall

[*See page* 20

OFF VALPARAISO IN 1921
Bound for Iquique in ballast

[*See page* 28

guano port, commonly called by sailors Pabellon de Pica, on the night of May 9, 1877.

The story is told in the following verses written by the late Rev. Canon R. J. Weatherhead, when chaplain to the Pacific Steam Navigation Company in Callao in 1877.

PABELLON DE PICA.

May 9, 1877.

Night spreads her sable mantle o'er the land;
The busy town is hushed; and sweet repose
Steals o'er the face of nature; naught is heard
Save the soft plash of waves upon the shore;
Or where a joyous party, mirth intent,
Make merriment, or on the anchored ship
The night watch pace the deck, or woman's voice
Is faintly heard, singing sweet songs of home.

But hark!
A sullen murmur strikes the ear;
Earth quakes and trembles, and the hills rain rocks;
A dozen fires in the doomed town burst forth,
Showing in lurid light th' affrighted folk
Panic-stricken in the street, and the ships
Tossing and whirling in the wild eddies
Of a maddened sea, and the hills trembling—
"La Mar! La Mar!" bursts from a hundred lips;
"The sea; the sea is coming!"

Great ocean
Draws into itself, like tiger springing
On its prey, and then in might appalling
Leaps upon the shore, and fire and water
Wage an elemental war, with horrid
Rumblings, and the shrieks of men and women,
And the shock of ships clashing together,
And the noise of houses crackling with flames,
Then buried hissing in the boiling surge!
Oh, God, how dread the scene!

Baffled, the sea
Retires 'tis but to spring, with fury fresh
And strength redoubled, on its face again;
And, wave on wave, incessant pouring,
Over the sunken ships it leaps to land,
And, heavenward rearing, rushes resistless
O'er all the prostrate town, beats down the flames.
House, ship and people, indiscriminate,
Sucks down its black abyss of yawning jaws
And in unfathom'd depths of darkness
Buries for shame the ruin it has wrought.

In the account of Mr. Perry, the captains and mates of the ships in port had assembled aboard the *C. F. Sargent* in order to bid good-bye to Captain Johnson of the *Independence*, according to the fashion of the coast. Three of the captains had wives and daughters, whilst Captain Johnson, besides two little girls, had a boy of eight. Most of the American officers hailed from the State of Maine, and after a farewell dinner many old-fashioned family games were played with the children until midnight, when the party broke up.

As Captain Johnson, with his wife and children, rowed away to his own ship, the rest of the party lined the rail of the *C. F. Sargent* and sang "Home, Sweet Home." The night was pitch dark and the air close and sultry. The voices of the singers broke a sort of unearthly stillness, which seemed to hang over the anchorage like a shroud. No sooner had the last notes died away than the night was again broken by the familiar sound of oars in their rowlocks, as the various captains and mates were pulled aboard their ships.

Barely half an hour later the first tremor of an earthquake caused wild screams ashore and the sudden rattle of chains in the hawse pipes from the anchorage, as every ship began to pay out cable in readiness for the dreaded tidal wave which nearly always accompanies West Coast earthquakes. When the wave rolled in a few moments later, all the ships were ready for it except the *Independence*, which was unable to pay out her cable fast enough owing to being fitted with an old-fashioned barrel windlass.

Let me quote Mr. Perry's vivid description of what happened:

> The cable jammed on the barrel, the hawse pipes were torn out, the chain cut through the planking far down below the load water-line, and instead of rising over the crest of the wave her bows were drawn under it as the wave swept her decks clean from stem to stern, carrying everything movable into the sea, and throwing the ship over on her beam ends, as she sheered sideways upon the returning wave.
>
> The water rushing in volumes through her uncaulked side ports and deck hatches quickly filled the hold below, and she began to settle rapidly, while nothing remained on deck but pieces of splintered boats, a few hatch covers, loose planks and gratings. The crew grasped anything that would sustain a human body and one by one dropped off into the sea and were carried away by the swirling waters.
>
> The captain, with the assistance of the ship's mate and carpenter, succeeded finally in unlashing the ship's gangway and getting it over the side. Upon this he placed his wife with the youngest child in her arms, and the nurse with the next older in her arms, then he followed with the boy clinging to his back. He grasped the side of the gangway as it slipped clear of the ship and went swirling off into the darkness, washed fore and aft by the seething sea. . . .
>
> . . . In this way they had drifted for some 15 minutes, which to them must have seemed hours, when suddenly out of the dark waters surrounding them appeared the hands, quickly followed by the head, of the Chinese steward struggling blindly towards them in his frantic efforts to find something to cling to before strength deserted him. As his hands clutched the already overloaded gangway, in his terror he attempted to draw his tired body over its rail for safety. The captain, scenting this new peril confronting them, worked his way laboriously towards him, and with superhuman effort grasped him by the throat and choked him, until the steward's hands gradually released their hold on the rail, and with a final gasp he disappeared under the dark surface of the sea.
>
> This was the last thing the captain remembered until he regained consciousness to find himself lying in one of the spare state-rooms of the *C. F. Sargent.*

Captain Johnson had been picked up by the "Sargent's" boat. When he had been found he was holding on to a heavy plank with one arm, whilst he still had a tight hold of his unconscious boy with the other.

The bodies of Mrs. Johnson, her two children, the stewardness, and the Chinese steward were found amongst the wreckage thrown up on the shore by the heavy surf which followed the tidal wave.

The Tragedy of the "Avonmore" at Huanillos.

The earthquake wave, which laid Pabellon de Pica in ruins, drowned numbers of its inhabitants, and sank the *Independence*, besides damaging most of the ships at the anchorage, played equal havoc at the little port of Huanillos, about 100 miles or so away.

The tragedy of the *Avonmore* at Huanillos is so like that of the *Independence* at Pabellon de Pica that the two have sometimes been confused, and I have seen it stated in print that the captain's wife was singing "Home, Sweet Home," in the cabin of the *Avonmore* at the actual moment when the tidal wave overwhelmed the ship.

The senior apprentice of the *Avonmore* is still alive and hearty, and the following is his account of the tragedy at Huanillos:

The *Avonmore* sailed from Cardiff coal laden for Monte Video in September, 1876. She was commanded by Captain Corfield, who had with him his wife and two children. She was manned by 32 hands all told, consisting of 17 A.B.'s and a bosun, all of whom where black men, and eight apprentices. After a light weather passage of 70 days the ship arrived at the

River Plate. Here the niggers skipped out and a very tough crowd were shipped in their place for the run round the Horn to Callao in ballast.

At Callao the *Avonmore* received orders to load guano at Huanillos. She arrived there on May 9, 1877, and anchored about 500 yards from the shore. It was a beautiful calm afternoon, with just the ordinary swell coming in. Twenty-six ships of various nationalities were lying at anchor in the open roadstead, the nearest being the ship *Geneva* of New York, loaded and hove short, ready to go to sea in the morning. Other ships close to the *Avonmore* were the *Goshawk* and *Sir Colin Campbell.*

Captain Corfield and his wife went ashore to get the ship's mail, and on their return the boat was hoisted up into the davits again. Thomas Hole, the senior apprentice, received a Bristol paper in the mail and was reading it in his bunk about 7·30 p.m., when the first slight shock was felt. This made the anchor chain surge somewhat, but little notice was taken of it. A few minutes later a second and third shock came along in rapid succession. Captain Corfield and the skipper of a Swansea barque who was dining with him came rushing out on to the quarter-deck, and the former at once ordered all hands to their stations. Hole sprang out of his bunk and ran aft to the wheel in order to reeve off the green hide wheel ropes which had been cast adrift. As soon as one side was rove off, the captain ordered him to put the wheel hard-a-port. By this time a tremendous confused sea was running, under the influence of which the *Avonmore* was gradually heeling over and over.

Before Hole left the wheel he saw the American ship

break from her moorings and go drifting by. About the same time also a Norwegian barque broke adrift and came down upon the *Avonmore*. For a moment it looked as if there would be a bad crash, then the Norwegian was by, having swept the *Avonmore's* boat out of the davits.

No sooner had the senior apprentice put the wheel hard-a-port than he was ordered down to the cabin by the mate, Mr. King, in order to help Mrs. Corfield and the stewardess (an Englishwoman from Newport, Monmouth) to put on their lifebelts. Between them they lashed the baby, which was only four months old, having been born during the voyage, on to the left side of the stewardess, and the boy of four years old on to his father's back. The other child was also lashed to the captain, being tied to the lifebelt on his chest.

These hurried preparations only took up a few moments, and then the whole party rushed up on deck, where, seeing the desperate state of things, the captain shouted out, "Every man for himself and God for us all!" The ship was gradually heeling over in the heavy sea. Most of the crew were forward working like madmen to launch the boats which were on the forward-house, but they only succeeded in getting one of them over the side before the *Avonmore* heeled right over and capsized.

As the ship turned bottom up Hole ran along the side, but he had not got far before he was washed off and went under, but he was a sturdy boy and not easily drowned. Striking out, he soon drove his head above water, and to his amazement found that he was alongside the actual keel of the vessel.

The tidal wave had evidently passed, and there was now a very strong suck or current rather than a heavy sea. Hole managed to cling to the keel and slip his trousers off before being again swept away. When he came to the surface again there was once more a heavy sea in addition to the current, which Lloyd's later reported as of 10-knot strength.

The apprentice found the sailmaker, an Irishman, in the water near him, and the latter shouted out, "Keep your head, Tom, and strike out!" The ship's dog, "Sailor," a retriever, was also swimming about near him, and not far away was the starboard lifeboat with ten or twelve men in her. Hole and the sailmaker shouted their best in order to draw the attention of those in the boat, but being without rowlocks it took them some time to reach the swimmers. Eventually the pair of them and the dog were all pulled safely into the boat.

The lifeboat, which had not been in the water for some time, was leaking badly, also the plug was out. Hole supplied the place of a plug with his thumb. With only his shirt on he declared that it was bitter cold in the boat. By this time it was also dark.

The next thing was what to do, whether to risk getting ashore through the surf, or to row out to sea, or to try to find one of the ships still at anchor. The discussion caused a great deal of lurid language amongst the mixed crew of nationalities who were in the boat, but it came to a sudden end when two boats belonging to the Bristol ship *Conference* arrived on the scene. The skipper of the *Conference* was aboard one of these, and he had managed to pick up Mr. King, the mate of the *Avonmore.*

Thomas Hole's tired thumb was now relieved by a wooden plug, three of the apprentices in the lifeboat were transferred into one of the *Conference* boats, whilst a bucket, a keg of fresh water, and some biscuits and matches were put aboard the leaky lifeboat. One of the *Conference* men kindly gave Hole, who was very cold and cramped after doing plug duty in the bottom of the boat, a pair of red woollen drawers, which the latter declared were a godsend.

The three boats now decided to pull out to sea, after agreeing to strike a match every ten minutes in order to keep company. The sea was by this time fairly calm, and the boats gradually drifted apart. At daybreak the *Avonmore's* lifeboat was still in sight of land, and the occupants immediately started pulling in towards it. After pulling for some time they eventually reached a Liverpool ship, one of the 23 ships which were still hanging to their moorings, though all of them were more or less damaged.

After receiving some food aboard the Liverpool ship, the lifeboat's crew decided to pull into the shore in order to report to the British Consul. The whole surface of the anchorage was covered with debris and wreckage, both from the ships and from the wharf. Amongst the floating bales and barrels they came across several pairs of ladies' stockings, whereupon the senior apprentice promptly drew a pair on to his bare legs in order to protect them from the hot sun, which was now scorching the backs of the lifeboat's crew. Another welcome bit of salvage was an 18-gallon barrel of French wine, which after a struggle they managed to get into the boat. The bung was hurriedly extracted, and with the aid of the bucket the shipwrecked men proceeded to dispose of its contents as quickly as possible.

As the boat neared the surf the crowd ashore warned them by every kind of signal that it was dangerous, but by this time the wine had filled all hands with unlimited courage, so they

VALPARAISO

Lent by C. A. Finsterbusch

See page 28

VALPARAISO IN A NORTHER, JUNE 2, 1903
Wrecks of "Foyledale" and "Chivilingo"

Lent by C. A. Finsterbusch

[*See page* 35

CALLAO

[See page 30

pulled in on top of the third wave. As the boat hit the beach with a crash her crew found themselves on their backs on the bottom boards. Luckily the shore folk were able to get hold of the painter and pull the boat clear before the next breaker arrived.

Leaving the boat and the barrel of wine in the hands of those who had pulled them out of the surf, the boat's crew hurried along the sands to where the bodies of a woman and a baby had been placed after being picked up on the sand. These proved to be the stewardess and the captain's baby. Thomas Hole has never forgotten the pitiful sight, and the shock sobered the crew of the lifeboat in a moment.

They were next told that a woman's body had been found three miles away along the shore. The apprentice and four others immediately set off to see if it was Mrs. Corfield. When they reached the body they had no difficulty in recognising it as that of their skipper's wife. Some ghouls had already stolen the rings off her fingers and the boots off her feet, but otherwise the body was uninjured.

They managed to find a window shutter, and placing the poor body upon it carried it back to the few ruins which represented the village of Huanillos after the earthquake and tidal wave had finished with it. Here they heard that Captain Corfield had been picked up alive by the crew of the American ship *New York*, but that the two boys lashed to him were both found to be dead. Upon hearing this news Hole, the sailmaker, and the three A.B.'s put the bodies of the skipper's wife, her baby, and the stewardess into the lifeboat and pulled off to the *New York*. Here they found their captain, who had the bodies of his wife and children packed in a large box of guano as a preservative. The *New York*, like all the rest of the ships at Huanillos and Pabellon de Pica, had to go to Callao for repairs, and Captain Corfield made an agreement with the American captain to take the bodies to Callao, where they were transferred in their box of guano to the British mail boat, which carried them home for burial.

Every ship, with the exception of the Swansea barque *Genesis*, which rode out the tidal wave at Huanillos, was compelled to slip her anchors as owing to the broken and disturbed state of the bottom they were so embedded that they could not be broken out.

The 3-ton longboat of the *Avonmore*, which her crew had just managed to launch off the top of the forward-house when the tidal wave struck the ship, was afterwards found half a mile inshore and quite undamaged.

Ashore, the stores, shanties, water tanks, condensing machinery and the "clink," with its solitary prisoner, were all overwhelmed and swept away by the first onrush of the tidal wave. Earthquake shocks of greater or less intensity were frequent for months afterwards, and often upset the new buildings with which the wretched natives were replacing their lost homes.

This account would not be complete without a few lines describing the subsequent adventures of Thomas Hole. As soon as he and the other four survivors had disposed of their sad burden they were at once taken charge of by the hard-hearted Yankee mate of the *New York*, who said that "he was not going to have them loafing around his decks doing nothing," and he turned them to along with his own crowd, who were sending down the light yards. It is probable that the *Avonmore* survivors were pretty well played out, and their slow, tired movements were so criticised by the Down East mate that at last Hole and his particular pal, another apprentice, went aft and told Captain Corfield that when they signed his indentures in Bristol it did not mean service under the U.S. flag or being cussed around by a bucko mate.

After some discussion, Captain Corfield arranged that Hole and his friend should be sent aboard the barque *Samuel* of London, which was also bound to Callao for repairs and was short-handed. The two lads immediately went aboard her and helped to heave her short ready for sea in the morning; but before the *Samuel* sailed from Huanillos Thomas Hole heard that the Swansea barque *Genesis* was a man short, and he immediately asked to be transferred to her as he knew her mate; and after a bit of palaver he was duly signed on aboard the Welshman at the port wages of £8 per month.

However, directly Captain Corfield heard of this arrangement he claimed Hole as a time-expired apprentice and acting third mate, and also as an essential witness with reference to the loss of the *Avonmore.* Hole therefore was sent back to the *Samuel,* whose skipper now declined to have him on board.

The apprentice was now in a fine quandary and found himself transferred from ship to ship for the next three or four months. The *Genesis* sailed, the *New York* sailed, the *Samuel* sailed, and each one in turn left the boy behind. At last, after Hole had spent some months partly ashore and partly on board different ships, another of Hill's Bristol ships arrived at Huanillos. This was *Her Royal Highness.* The apprentice at once went aboard and explained his queer position. He was signed on and taken home in that vessel, which took a cargo of guano to Antwerp.

After being nearly twelve months on this tragic and sun-scorched island since the loss of his ship, we may be sure that Thomas Hole was not sorry when he saw the last of it sink below the horizon.

The Great Valparaiso Earthquake.

A curious fact about the great Valparaiso earthquake of August 16, 1906, was that the sea seems to have been very slightly affected. There were, however, one or two unusual phenomena, which may or may not have been caused by the earthquake.

From the extreme South to the Bay of Arauco nothing unusual was noted, though a norther blew further South at Corral which made observations difficult. In the port of Coronel high waves and a cross sea rolled up immediately after the quake, but there was no wind. Mr. Juan Jones, who lived close to the shore, noted, however, that there was a great uproar in the harbour, with thundering noises.

At Talcahuano at 8.15 p.m. there was a distinct ebb and flow of the sea. The water went back 50 to 60 metres from the shore, then flooded in quietly again. The captain of the port reported that the ebb was extreme, with an unusually low run. The same thing happened at Tomé and Penco, where the vagaries of the tide caused considerable alarm. At Constitucion the tide flooded about 3 ft. 4 ins. higher than usual, and a bore ran up the River Maule. Here many people noted what they described as the hoarse roaring of the sea, with occasional detonations.

A steamer passing Sant' Antonio observed a brilliant yellow glare on the western horizon, whilst for some distance around the water appeared to be boiling, as if from the effect of a submarine volcano. Along the coast where the "terremoto" was strongest, there was no disturbance of the water at the time of the quake, though some time later the sea became confused and angry.

In the Bay of Valparaiso itself the quietness of the sea during and immediately after the earthquake was quite remarkable, yet it was generally agreed by both the scientists and seafarers, such as the coast fishermen, that the coastline had been raised about 2 feet above its old level extending from the River Mataquito in the South to the River Choapa in the North, which was the zone of the earthquake's greatest intensity.

It may perhaps be of interest to give some slight account of this terrible cataclysm which laid Valparaiso in ruins.

On August 16, 1906, although the signs of approaching spring were clearly to be seen in the hinterland, at Valparaiso the weather was still quite wintry. Along the water-front thousands of people were enjoying themselves in bars, restaurants, and music-halls. Suddenly, at about 7.56 p.m. the earth began to dance and shake as if it had gone mad. Mr. Krahnass, of the National Observatory at Santiago, gave the time of the first quake, as taken with his chronometer, at 7.58.36, and Mr. Greave, the astronomer, agreed with this within a second or two.

The quake was simultaneous at Santiago and Valparaiso. This was proved by two ladies, who were having a conversation over the telephone and at the same moment cried out "Tiembla" ("It trembles").

The panic-stricken people immediately rushed out into the streets and open places. The heaving of the ground was so strong for four minutes that it was impossible to stand up. The oscillations seemed to come from every point of the compass and the actual surface of the earth jumped up and down with such force that heavy benches and seats in the open places were flung about in every direction, whilst telegraph and telephone poles actually jumped clean out of the ground and came down with a crash. Traffic, of course, stopped at the instant, and trams were crushed as the whole front of big stone houses fell out upon them, followed by showers of tiles from the roofs of the buildings.

All over the city the thundering noise and crash of falling towers and houses mingled with the cries of the panic-stricken population. To add to the horror and confusion the electric light went out all over the city with the first quake and left it in complete darkness, which, however, was rendered even more horrible by a kind of blood-red glow in the heavens and the electric flashes caused by short circuits.

The heavy quakes lasted for a full four minutes, but tremors of every description continued at intervals throughout the night and for many days afterwards. It has never been ascertained how many people were killed during those first tragic four minutes. Some said thousands, others tens of thousands. The number of dead dug out from the ruins by the authorities was kept secret.

At the end of the four minutes there was a sudden terror-filled silence. The half-stunned survivors could see nothing owing to the dense blackness of the night, which blotted out the ruins of the city. Then the fire from open gas pipes, kitchen stoves, paraffin lamps, etc., began. First a glare here, another there, then five, then twenty, and finally a sea of flames. Valparaiso was afire, and in a few moments dense clouds of smoke mingled with the dust which had risen into the air from the stricken city.

People ran hither and thither, some crying for help, some screaming with fear, some shouting the names of their missing relations; numbers of frenzied men and women rushed from the shore towards the hills in order to get away from the expected tidal wave. Others put out from the land in order to seek safety aboard the ships, but, as I have already said, the dreaded sea of Valparaiso, which year after year makes sport of the city with its terrible northers, remained placid and quiet throughout the night, the smiling water reflecting the fires of the Almendral, Puerto, Bellavista, and Baron, and also those from the surrounding hills Cordillera, Concepcion, and others.

No ship came to grief, not even a lighter was grounded or a row-boat stove in. The terror struck at the land alone, but the fist of fate fell with such fury upon the unlucky port of Valparaiso that the town was first reduced to a rubble of bricks and mortar and then burnt.

The seamen aboard the ships in the Bay were, however, roused from their sleep by the tremendous quake, which actually shook the ships from stem to stern. Tumbling pell-mell out of their bunks officers dashed on deck in their pyjamas, blowing their whistles and calling for all hands on deck in expectation of the usual tidal wave. They were in time to see the great semi-circle of thousands of lights around the water's edge and the arcs of electric light on the hills, which resembled a huge swarm of fireflies, suddenly go out and leave the city shrouded in a dense black pall of dust. Then across the water came the noise of the crash of falling buildings, the cries of the terrified inhabitants, and above all the terrible roar of the cataclysm as it heaved and fell deep down under the surface of the earth. Then came the lurid yellow glare of the fires.

Immediately from every ship landing parties were organised to go to the help of the stricken city. At first there was a good deal of unavoidable confusion; steamers blew their sirens, and tug-boats whistled, with the vague idea of drawing every ship's attention to the horror ashore. Then the warships anchored at the Torpederas and naval depots trained their searchlights upon the shore and revealed the whole terror of the catastrophe. The town of Valparaiso seemed to have gone —vanished—until nothing but heaps of bricks remained.

Then Admiral Gomez Carreno, the Commander of the port, hurriedly organised the salvage work. The fire was fought not only by hundreds of fire-engines, but by the pumps of the tugs and other vessels. Meanwhile the police, aided by the seamen of the Chilian Navy, began to take energetic action against the human hyenas who were already prowling about the debris of the broken buildings under the cover of darkness and robbing the dead and the wounded of their money and jewellery. Everywhere in amongst the wreckage bands of seamen from the shipping in port worked heroically amongst the ruins rescuing men, women and children from the remains of their shattered homes.

From the scientific point of view the catastrophe was characterised by a complete absence of instrumental records. At the first quake the seismograph of the National Observatory

IQUIQUE IN 1903
Ships "Calliope," "Alsterkamp," "Kondor"
Lent by the Nautical Photo Agency [See page 54

LOADING BRIDGE, ANTOFAGASTA

Lent by the Nautical Photo Agency

SAILING SHIPS AT PISAGUA.

jumped from its seat and was rendered useless, and the same thing happened with all the other instruments.

Further away, however, scientists received plenty of information from their instruments, which registered the earthquake as far East as Buenos Aires, as far North as Tacna, and as far South as Quemchi in the department of Ancud in latitude 42° 10′ S. At the island of Juan Fernandez, which was about 360 miles from the affected region, there was a stiff South-west gale during the night, with heavy rain, thunder and lightning. Seismic tides due to the Valparaiso earthquake were afterwards reported from the Hawaii Islands. Mr. Milne, of the Magnetic Observatory of Pilar in Cordoba, Argentina, reported that his instruments showed an uninterrupted series of tremors varying in intensity for a total duration of 2 hours 34 minutes. At Santiago, Mr. Krahnass, of the National Observatory, stated that the duration of the quake was 4 minutes 50 seconds, and that it started with moderate oscillations and after an interval assumed a tremendous intensity. The lighthouse keeper of Punta Curaumilla reported that the shock there was extremely sudden, violent and without interval. Mr. A. Holmgren, director of the Pilot School, who was aboard the frigate *Abtao*, at anchor before Coquimbo, declared that there were two strong shocks with a 5-minute interval, and that the shocks had two distinct periods of intensity.

In earthquakes the scientists place a great importance on the direction of the oscillations. As regards the Valparaiso earthquake the reports from the various points along the coast were very contradictory. It was agreed that at Valparaiso and in the neighbourhood the oscillations were not only from North to South and from East to West, but even perfectly vertical, this vertical motion being so intense that heavy objects were actually flung into the air from the ground.

As regards the intensity of the earthquake, the scientists agreed that it reached the maximum ever recorded, grade 10 in the scale, though of course some parts of the town were less affected than others.

The above account of the Valparaiso earthquake has been taken from the reports of Dr. H. Steffen, the newspaper *El Mercurio*, and from the personal reminiscences of some of the survivors.

Sailing Ships at Valparaiso during the Earthquake.

It may be of interest to give the names of the sailing ships which were in port at Valparaiso on the day of the earthquake:

The *Thetis*, British barque, which had arrived in the Bay on April 9, sailed from Valparaiso on the very day, August 16; and the *Queen Mab*, British barque, actually arrived during the earthquake, being 66 days out from Newcastle, N.S.W.

The vessels in port were:

Ben Lee, British ship, which arrived June 29, 62 days from Newcastle, N.S.W.
Bertha, German barque, which arrived July 1, 91 days from Hamburg.
Bessfield, British barque, which arrived August 3, 63 days from Newcastle, N.S.W.
Criccieth Castle, British ship, which arrived June 21, 47 days from Newcastle, N.S.W.
Dunreggan, British barque, which arrived June 18, 51 days from Newcastle, N.S.W.
Halewood, British ship, which arrived June 3, 61 days from Newcastle, N.S.W.
John Cooke, British ship, which arrived June 3, 57 days from Melbourne.
Musselcrag, British barque, which arrived June 13, 61 days from Newcastle, N.S.W.
Palmyra, German ship, which arrived August 9, 100 days from Hamburg.
Pamelia, German barque, which arrived July 31, 96 days from Antwerp.
Pax, British barque, which arrived June 25, 62 days from Tacoma.
Posen, German ship, which arrived June 26, 80 days from Hamburg.
Seestern, German barque, which arrived July 21, 78 days from Port Blakely.
Sir Robert Fernie, British barque, which arrived June 11, 73 days from Chemainus.
Swanhilda, British barque, which arrived August 3, 37 days from Newcastle, N.S.W.

Teresa, Italian barque, which arrived June 4, 77 days from Newcastle, N.S.W.
Thekla, German barque, which arrived June 13, 49 days from Newcastle, N.S.W.
Wandsbek, German barque, which arrived June 13, 68 days from Port Blakely.

The following vessels also were probably in the port during the earthquake:

Biagio O, Italian ship, arrived May 12, left Iquique October 2.
Cambrian Monarch, British ship, arrived April 29, sold to Chile.
Caterina Bianchi, Italian ship, arrived June 14, sailed from Iquique November 10.
Cristobel Soler, Chilian ship, arrived March 15.
Erna, German barque, arrived July 1, reached Antofagasta from Valparaiso August 20.
Gwyder Castle, British barque, arrived July 6, sailed from Tocopilla October 24.
Invincible, American ship, arrived May 24, reported arrived Port Townsend October 30.
Persimmon, German barque, arrived June 13, sailed from Tocopilla September 7.

Northers.

Next to the tidal wave the greatest danger to shipping on the W.C.S.A. is the norther, which sweeps down upon the open anchorages, and is specially to be feared in the Bay of Valparaiso. These northers, as a rule, give sufficient warning for sailing ships to look to their ground tackle, and for steamers to get up steam and gain an offing. Sometimes, however, the norther was too much for the stoutest cables, and when such an anchorage as that of Valparaiso or Iquique was crowded with shipping a great deal of damage was done by the ships crashing into each other.

Probably the worst norther experienced on the West Coast since the beginning of the twentieth century was that of June 2, 1903, when the British full-rigged ship *Foyledale,* the Chilian barque *Chivilingo,* and the P.S.N.Co. coast steamer *Arequipa* were lost. The barometer had been slowly falling for several days previous to the 2nd, and everyone in Valparaiso knew that a norther was imminent. The *Foyledale,* which had lately arrived from Portland (Oregon), with a cargo of lumber consigned to Grace & Co., was moored in the tier nearest the shore, close to the Baron Station. This berth was never an ideal anchorage in the wintertime, as there was always a considerable backwash.

All day Monday, June 1, there was so much sea in the bay that the lighters discharging the shipping could hardly work. By sunset the wind was blowing hard from the dreaded quarter, and a drenching rain had began to fall. At midnight the wind was blowing in hurricane gusts. It was pitch dark and bitterly cold, and great seas were rolling into the "malecon." The tremendous surf hurling itself against the embankment tossed huge stones, great logs of timber, heavy iron pipes and all kinds of merchandise across the railway line and against the houses and "bodegas" in the Avenida Errazuriz. Even the heavy hydraulic cranes were torn from their places. Soon the whole "malecon" front was littered with debris of all sorts, whilst the Bellavista Station was water-logged, and the Plaza Bellavista and the Calle Blanco were blocked with slabs of timber, bales of "pasto," broken pieces of "flatero" boats, and innumerable floating cans of paraffin. The watchers ashore were compelled to keep their distance, as no one could stand against the great clouds of spray which swept the front.

Towards morning the anxious watchers saw rockets piercing the blackness of the night out to sea, and even could distinguish whistles and cries above the roaring of the winds and the thunder of the sea; but no help could be given to the shipping until daylight.

The Wreck of the "Foyledale."

The *Foyledale* was a fine full-rigged ship of 1666 tons owned by John Porter and others. Her master, Captain Kerry, was a very experienced seaman, but as it was his first visit to Valparaiso he was obliged to be satisfied with the berth awarded him by the port authorities.

The *Foyledale,* moored with two anchors ahead and two astern, with about 75 fathoms on each, hung on well in the heavy backwash until about 3 a.m., when the starboard cable carried away at the keelson. After some terrific work in the pitch darkness, the crew of the *Foyledale* managed to get a big spring on to the cable and make it fast round the foremast. Soon after this, however, the ship began to drag, and Captain Kerry at once realised that she was doomed and that it was unlikely that anyone aboard would live through the night.

Only those who have gone through such an experience can realise the agony of mind suffered by Captain Kerry that night, for in the cabin of the *Foyledale* were his young wife and little daughter Eileen.

At 3 a.m., when the starboard cable went, he jumped below for a moment and told his wife that she had better dress as they might have to make an attempt to reach the shore at any minute. Mrs. Kerry was very brave, and after praying for the ships in the bay and that the remaining anchor would hold, stayed quietly in the saloon reading to her daughter.

At 4 a.m., when the ship started to drag, Captain Kerry again came below and told his wife that it was time for them to come on deck. After making them put on their warmest clothing he embraced his wife and child before leading the way to the deck. The little girl, who had seen many a gale of wind, was quite unaware of the danger, and as they went up the companion-way, called out "Are we going ashore now? Hurrah for Valparaiso!"

Hardly were the words out of her mouth before the chart-house, into which the stairway led, was torn away over their heads, and they had their breath taken away by a shower-bath of icy cold spray. The little girl, in her father's arms, gave a whimper of fright, but her mother cried out bravely, "It will soon be daylight, and then we will go ashore," and she even attempted to sing a few lines of the child's favourite hymn, "Light in the darkness, sailor, day is at hand."

By this time the ship was being swept by heavy seas, and all hands, after having been mustered on the poop, had been compelled to take refuge in the mizen rigging. Before getting into the rigging with his wife and daughter, Captain Kerry handed little Eileen over to her devoted friend, the second mate, Alfred George, who swore that he would never let her go whilst life was in him. Mrs. Kerry followed the second mate up the ratlines, the captain keeping close behind her with his arms round her. Unfortunately they were not able to get up very far owing to the men above them, and thus the spray from every sea drenched them, and even solid water did its best to tear them from the rigging.

Soon after this some of the logs composing the *Foyledale's* deck cargo broke adrift from their lashings and pounded against the main and fore masts with such force that these two masts speedily went by the board. At this the mate, who was a real good man, climbed down out of the mizen rigging and made for the shelter of the wheelhouse, which was a brand new addition that voyage. He left the mizenmast because he felt sure that it would follow the fore and main over the side, but this mistake in judgment cost him his life, for he was caught by the backwash swirling over the counter and swept away. In a short time the ship began bumping on the rocks, and these bumps, together with the blows received from the gigantic surf, threatened to break the hold of the exhausted crew in the mizen rigging. As soon as they realised that the ship was up on the beach the seamen began crying out for help, and voices ashore could be heard through the darkness replying to them, for there were only 70 yards between the ship and dry land; but those 70 yards were 70 yards of white water, through which no man could pass alive.

It was now about 5 a.m., and the captain's wife who, for the past hour, had been trying to cheer up her husband and encourage the men in the rigging above her, began to grow exhausted, and her brave voice gradually grew fainter until it could no longer be heard. The captain, who had been taking the weight of every sea on his broad back, was in a like state, dazed and choked by salt water and almost beaten senseless.

About this time the second mate, with the little Eileen in his arms, climbed down the rigging and made a desperate attempt to clear the short distance between the ship and the shore. Both Captain Kerry and his wife heard the faint cry of their daughter as she went under, and though nothing could be seen in the darkness they both realised that their child had been taken from them.

Another account states that the second mate and his little charge were knocked out of the rigging by a huge sea with a mass of lumber on its crest, which brought him to the deck, and that he got to his feet with the child still in his arms, but was carried away by the next sea, never to be seen alive again.

For perhaps half an hour longer Captain Kerry remained conscious. Then, whilst there was still no sign of the dawn, a heavy breaker swept through the shrouds, tore his wife from his arms and knocked him insensible. One of the seamen, however, Healy by name, managed to lash the captain to the shrouds with the end of a buntline, at the risk of his own life, for by this time every breaker swept over the wreck to the height almost of the mizen top.

As soon as it was light enough to see anything, those who were still hanging in the rigging noticed that the lumber cargo was being forced out of the main hatch by the sea, and for a few moments a bridge between the ship and the shore was formed by the timber and planks. Four of the most active men in the crew managed to scramble on to the rocks by means of this bridge, although they were somewhat knocked about and had to be bound up in the "salvavida's" house, which happened to be right opposite the wreck. One of the apprentices, who tried to follow their example, was either killed or drowned between the planking and the ship.

Soon after daylight the rocket apparatus, which the men in the rigging had been calling for for so long, was got ready, and a line fired off. The first shot went wide. The second was caught by one of the men in the rigging, but he was obliged to let go. The third shot, however, was successful, but it was nearly 7 a.m. before the block and tackle were made fast to the mast and the guiding line held by two gangs of volunteers.

The lines had to be very carefully tended as the ship lay almost broadside on to the surf, and as each breaker burst against her the *Foyledale* was rocked violently from side to side, thus tautening and slackening the lifeline. By the time that the first of those in the rigging, an apprentice, was got into the cradle ready for hauling ashore, a huge crowd had gathered. There was a sudden hush, and even the shrieking of the wind seemed to be lessened as the strain was put on the rope, and the apprentice in the cradle was slowly hauled towards the shore.

The men on the hauling line pulled as steadily and smoothly as they could, but just when the boy was halfway to the shore a tremendous breaker swept high over the ship and listed her shorewards. Then, as she righted again through the strength of the backwash, the rope was tightened with a jerk which took the men upon it by surprise, so that they were unable to pay out quick enough. The strain on the lifeline increased until the rope snapped, and the boy in the cradle fell on to the floating wood which was tossing about between the ship and the shore. Luckily the rope had broken on the ship side of the cradle, so that the boy was still connected with the shore.

One of the four men who had already been saved now dashed into the sea with a rope round his waist and managed to reach the apprentice. After being washed up against the rocks by the surf the two were hauled to safety.

It is a little difficult for the reader to visualise this scene of rescue. Opposite the ship, on the railway line, a train of ballast cars, loaded with blocks of granite, which were being used for the repair of the "malecon," were crowded with excited spectators, who shrieked out advice at one moment and howled with lamentation the next, as they watched the efforts of the life-saving crew. It was bitterly cold, and every sea as it raced ashore swept clean over the *Foyledale* and over the men clinging in her rigging, and everybody ashore began to wonder how long those men would be able to hang on.

As soon as the apprentice, who was bleeding profusely from the mouth, was carried off to be administered to by a doctor in the crowd, every voice besought the commandante to fire his cannon again in order to re-establish communication with the ship. But the commandante was half frenzied with indecision. He only had one more cartridge. His rocket apparatus was broken and in danger of bursting, and if he missed his aim it was certain death to those in the rigging.

Advice and vituperation were showered on the wretched commandante by the excited crowd, and in the end he was persuaded to fire his last shot. The aim was a good one, and the line fell right over the mast, which drew a great "Viva!" from the crowd.

The hawser was now dragged across the surf by the salvage corps, and luckily, one of the men in the rigging, a young fellow with a shock of yellow hair, had sufficient strength to climb up and make it fast, according to instructions shouted through a speaking trumpet.

Apparently neither cradle nor breeches buoy was available, and the survivors in the rigging were compelled to make their way hand over hand along the hawser. This was no easy job, for at one moment, as the ship heeled, the hawser would be dipped into the surf, and at the next, with a jerk be raised 30 to 40 feet in the air. Only an acrobat or a sailor could have hung on under such conditions, and the first man who attempted it would undoubtedly have fallen into the sea owing to his strength giving out, if the man who had plunged into the surf to save the apprentice had not gone to the rescue with a rope round his waist, and caught the exhausted seaman as the hawser dipped him into the sea. Thus the man was hauled out, badly bruised and extremely exhausted, but otherwise little the worse.

Let me now quote the account given to the local newspaper by one of those who witnessed the saving of the *Foyledale's* crew.

From this man I learnt that the captain, if not dead, was insensible, and as we looked across that seething space it seemed so, for whilst his arms and legs appeared twisted through the rigging, his head hung listlessly downwards. I was also informed that one of the crew had had his legs broken or badly damaged. A second individual now came hand over hand along the rope. This man had taken the precaution to support his body with a line attached to the hawser, and though his journey was also perilous and he was subjected to dippings and tossings, there was not the same fear of his not reaching the shore.

As it was still necessary for someone to go aboard, I turned to the Britisher beside me (the man who had dashed into the surf to save the apprentice and the other man), and he again expressed his willingness to go, but just then I was delighted to see the "salvavida" men coming along with the rope which had been clamoured for for so long, and to it was fixed a block, tackle and pulley with cradle suspended. The block and tackle were tied on the hawser, and instructions shouted to the men in the rigging to haul away. Whilst all were willing, owing to their being disabled and benumbed, their assistance was rather spasmodic, but the little fellow in the topmast position with a shock of yellow hair—a Dane, I believe—did yeoman service. He seemed to hang on only with his teeth until the block and tackle were within his reach.

Attached to the block was a board with instructions, but I anathematised the useless rocket apparatus when I found the instructions were only in Spanish. A Chilian gentleman now came forward and offered to send a pencil message. However, the sailor rigged the gear properly.

Out of the tremendous multitude the volunteers were now divided into four sections. Those in the railway cars held the hawser tight, or eased up as the motion of the ship and sea indicated. The section on the left stood waiting to haul the guiding line and cradle to shore, and the fourth section stood on the front, close to the water's edge, directing the working of the guiding lines, and ready to rescue the distressed seamen as they approached the rocks.

A man dropped into the cradle, and on the signal being given, one line was paid and the other hauled in. The excitement was intense; but, alas, with a groan it was noticed that the cradle had almost dropped down to the deck of the vessel and the waves were dashing over it. By following shouted instructions the men on the right side hauled in their line once more, and to our great relief we found that the cradle was in its old position.

Instinctively almost, the method of working the apparatus was now grasped and there were no more hitches. As the cradle came slowly to shore one great and prolonged cheer was sent up from the crowd. As soon as one unfortunate was brought ashore, and with a great deal of hazard extricated from the canvas cradle, for with the straining of the ship the cradle was being tossed constantly and forcibly into the air, the cradle was hauled out again, and another man took his place in the breeches buoy.

In this way all the survivors were brought ashore, with the exception of the yellow-headed Dane and the captain. The Dane made an attempt to get the captain into the cradle, but he was too exhausted and was obliged to leave his commander and get into the cradle himself. As soon as "yellowhead" was safely landed two of the life-saving corps, Alejandro Valverde and Manuel Casanova, volunteered to be hauled out to the ship in order to save the captain. They found it impossible to get the insensible man into the cradle, and eventually he was hauled ashore slung in a bowline made fast under his armpits. Captain Kerry did not regain consciousness until nearly 1 p.m.

In addition to the captain's wife and child and the second mate, the mate, carpenter, steward and two apprentices were drowned in this tragic shipwreck.

As regards the Chilian barque *Chivilingo*, her crew were all saved with the exception of the sailmaker and the cook.

The greatest loss of life occurred on the *Arequipa*. Captain Todd ordered steam to be got up and all to be ready for sea by 2 a.m. on the 2nd, but before the ship could get away from her berth the big stern mooring buoys crashed through the stern as she was thumped down upon them by the seas. The order had been given to go slow ahead, but after the propeller had given a few turns there was a fearful scrunching noise and the engines stopped. It was at once perceived that the ship was in desperate danger, for she had sheered broadside on to the sea with a heavy list, whilst every wave poured into her stokehold and engine-room.

Captain Todd immediately gave orders for life-belts to be served out and for the boats to be got ready, whilst rockets and blue lights were burnt and the siren blown. But there was no hope of any help from the shore on such a night, and aboard the steamer there was a great deal of confusion and panic amongst the passengers. There were at least 100 people on board, and, as the ship dipped her starboard rail under in an ever steeper list, these all crowded on to the port side of the bridge deck. The water rose in the engine-room until the fires were put out, and at 5.31 the *Arequipa* suddenly began to sink by the stern.

Out of the 100 people on board only 20 were saved by the gallant efforts of boats from the ships, *Laurel Branch, Poltalloch,* and *Titania.* Amongst those drowned was the captain's wife, in accordance with that dreadful law, or perhaps one should call it superstition, of the sea.

Other casualties during that terrible night were the foundering of the Government dredger *Holanda* near the Prat pier with the loss of one life, the collision of the German ship *Persimmon* with one of the floating docks, both ship and dock being damaged, and the wrecking of over 30 small boats and lighters.

The Bay of Valparaiso has been the scene of many an heroic deed which has gone unrecorded by the Press, for often at the height of a norther the men of sinking ships have been saved by the lifeboats of other vessels which were in almost as bad a plight themselves.

Let me try to reconstruct one of these gallant rescues. A norther is blowing with hurricane squalls, and the Bay of Valparaiso is a smother of foam and spindrift. The ships, with springs on their cables, are plunging bows under. (On more than one occasion it happened that the heavy capstan was torn from its bed and even hurled over the side by the furious jerking of the cables.) The crew of each ship may be seen "standing by" on the poop, the captain, perhaps, with his wife and children by his side. Then night comes on, and the stars and even the moon are shrouded in a veil of rain and salt water which is as impenetrable as the blackest fog.

Slowly the night passes until of a sudden a rocket hisses into the sky and bursts, to be quickly followed by another and another. This is a signal either that a ship is dragging her anchors or else is in danger of foundering. At once there is a stir on the nearest ships, the lifeboats are swung out, and a crew of volunteers with cork jackets strapped on take their places on the thwarts and are lowered into the water. Many a boat is crushed against the side of the ship and her crew thrown into the water before they can push off, but usually two or three of these gallant boat's crews succeed in getting alongside the ship in distress and taking off her company.

Such work, in the pitch darkness, the flying scud, and the mountainous seas, carried out by deep-waterman who were as a rule nothing wonderful as boatmen, deserved a jugful of Albert medals, but, as is the way with the sea, the greatest reward these heroes ever received was a tot of grog.

In the norther of July, 1905, over 30 lives were saved by ships' boats from vessels which were in imminent danger themselves. This gale did immense damage along the coast, six ships being driven ashore and some 60 lives being lost.

Fun on the Coast.

It must not be supposed that West Coast traders spent their time riding over tidal waves or weathering out northers. As a rule the ships lay peacefully on their anchors whilst the pitch melted in the deck seams.

Apprentices especially had a good time. During working days they usually had the afternoon ashore, their job being to row the captain to the landing stage and wait there until he had done his business. On Saturdays and Sundays it was the custom in many ports for the skippers to make up a fishing party. You do not fish with hook and eye on the West Coast but with sticks of dynamite. The usual procedure was for the boats to make a ring in some shallow inlet, and then for a small bomb to be thrown into the water which would explode as soon as it touched the bottom and send up a shower of fish which were stunned and floated for a minute or two on their backs insensible. The apprentices in the circle of boats were all provided with nets of the butterfly or shrimping type, and with these they dipped out the fish until their boats were almost full. Some captains who were keen naturalists used to go away for two or three days in a ship's boat with half a dozen apprentices exploring the coast on the lookout for rare birds and fish.

One can hardly imagine a more enjoyable expedition for adventurous boys, and many a present-day captain of a palatial liner must remember his old care-free days in the half-deck of a West Coast trader, and those fishing and shooting expeditions, with a longing to be back in his teens—a sunburnt, bare-footed, hard-muscled son of the sea.

The only idea of fun possessed by the average member of a sailing ship's foc's'le was of course the grog shop and the fandango house. His rollicking liberty day was usually followed by a night spent in an insect-infested "calaboose," where he had plenty of time to sober up whilst his skipper was paying the fine which would, in due course, be deducted from his scanty pay.

The West Coast was a veritable paradise for drunkards. In the old days one could buy five treepas of aquardiente for a dollar. These treepas were long sausage-shaped wine skins of two sizes, called one and two bottle treepas. They were very handy for smuggling drink aboard a ship, for one could carry a small treepa round one's waist in the bight of one's shirt above the waistband, or suspended down a trouser leg, up a shirt sleeve, or even coiled inside one's headgear.

Many and many a good British seaman deserted in such ports as Valparaiso or Callao owing to the attraction of cheap drink. He then either drifted into the ranks of the beachcombers or developed a business head and became the successful proprietor of a fandango hall or sailors' boarding-house.

Numbers of European seamen served for a term in the Chilian Navy. Many of the Chilian warships in the olden days were three-quarters manned by wild foreign sailormen of every nationality, and in order to preserve some semblance of discipline in such a rabble, old-fashioned punishments had to be resorted to until long after they had been given up by other

"PAMPA"

[*See page* 61

"PARCHIM"

Lent by Captain Lee

[*See page* 63

"POSEN" (TAKEN IN THE DOLDRUMS)

[*See page* 62

navies. The chief trouble of course was drink, and after a pay-day, which as I have already stated was a somewhat rare occurrence, the whole spar deck of a Chilian gunboat had often to be converted into a "brig." Each broadside gun had a couple of drunks married to it in this fashion—each man was lashed by the ankles and wrists to those of his opposite number, one being on each side of the gun—and there they were left to sober up as best they could.

This was a comparatively light punishment. Besides flogging, the old-fashioned method of dipping from the yardarm was frequently resorted to in the Chilian Navy until more or less recent days. The prisoner in this case was slung in a bowline and trussed with stops to the rope until he could move neither hand nor foot. Then with a stamp and go to the tune of the bosun's pipe, he was hauled up to the main yardarm, a toggle in the rope just above his head preventing him from cracking his skull on the gantline block.

As soon as he was up the pipe trilled out "Belay." The men on the rope did not turn it over a pin, but just stopped. For a moment the prisoner hung suspended, then the pipes of the bosun's mates shrilled out together "Let go," and down he dropped like a plummet, and, as the sailors say, "bored a hole in the water."

The next call was "walk away," and out he came dripping from the depths. The usual punishment was to dip a man three times, and its effect on a drunkard must have been very health-restoring.

The "Caleuche."

No book dealing with the history of shipping on the West Coast of South America would be complete without some mention of the *Caleuche*, the famous phantom ship which has long been the terror of Chilote sailors.

My attention was drawn to this modern *Flying Dutchman* by a letter which I received from Chile in August, 1929. That letter stated that the missing Danish training-ship, *Kobenhavn*, had been sighted off the South-west Coast followed by the dreaded *Caleuche.*

It may be remembered that the great five-masted training-ship, which was built at Leith, went missing in the spring of 1929. The *Kobenhavn* left Monte Video in ballast on December 14, 1928, bound for Melbourne and the last wireless message from her was received on December 21, when she was 400 miles East of the River Plate. Just a month later a large vessel was sighted by the islanders of Tristan da Cunha, about nine miles off and heading straight for the island.

The day was wild and stormy with a high wind blowing. The strange vessel was steering due North on a course which looked like landing her on the beach. The sight caused great excitement amongst the 150 odd souls on the lonely island. It was soon apparent that the great ship was badly down by the stern, and that her mainmast was missing. She had all her canvas snugly furled except for one of her lower topsails, and it soon became evident that she was derelict—that there was not a soul aboard. As the vessel approached various details could easily be distinguished which identified her with the *Kobenhavn*, the most important of which was perhaps the colouring of her hull—black with a broad white band.

When the stranger was within a quarter of a mile of the rocky shore, the run of the tide evidently caught her and carried her round the West Point of the island. Right in her new course a reef of barely submerged rocks extends out about a mile and a half from the shore and the islanders were certain that she could not have cleared this obstacle though no one saw her strike, and she seems to have been lost in the haze.

No more was seen of the derelict, but a few days afterwards a large punt and what was recognised as a machine-gun cover were washed up in the surf. These had no identification marks of any sort. For some months this story seemed to give the clue to the mystery of the missing training-ship—then the Finnish barque, *Ponape*, on arrival in Australia, reported that she had passed Tristan da Cunha on January 21.

As the desolate islands of the Southern Ocean have all been searched in vain for traces of the *Kobenhavn*, most seamen now consider that ice may have been the cause of the tragedy. That the great ship has been seen shewn up in the glare of the dreaded *Caleuche* only goes to prove to every superstitious seafarer that she is no more.

We owe most of our knowledge of the *Caleuche* to the inhabitants of Chiloe, who have been going to sea as coasting traders, fishermen and whalers from time immemorial.

The island of Chiloe remained an untouched Spanish stronghold for some time after the rest of Chile had freed itself from the yoke of Spain—until indeed the Government declared it a province of the Republic. The Chilotes thus are considered different to the other Chileans, not up-to-date and sunk in superstitution. They are undoubtedly very psychic and their belief in their own peculiar phantom ship, the *Caleuche*, cannot be shaken.

This *Flying Dutchman* of the Chilean coast apparently has no particular rig; though usually it is described as a vessel of old-fashioned design, bluff bowed, high sterned and square rigged. Very often it resembles one of the native craft, which have short stumpy masts in order to withstand the stormy weather of Southern Chile, or a small coasting "goleta" or schooner, but it has also been reported under many other rigs.

Its one invariable characteristic is its luminous appearance, which on a black night is like a blaze of light as if of a ship on fire. Fishermen, caught off shore in bad weather and riding it out to a sea anchor, have declared that they have seen the blazing *Caleuche,* with every spar and sail outlined by yellow flames, heading dead into the wind's eye as they crouched in the bottom of their tossing whaleboat.

It is usually under full sail and heads in any direction, taking no heed of wind or sea or even rocks. As a rule it is only seen at night though there are a few instances of it showing up just before dusk, transparent and faintly luminous against the glow of the setting sun or the rising moon. It is, of course, best seen against a blue-black midnight sky. It is never seen in rainy or snowy weather, but always just before or during a hard gale of wind. Then its appearance is considered very unlucky, involving those who have seen it in almost certain destruction. Occasionally they escape for a time only to meet their doom later.

There are of course the usual grisly additions to this ghost ship such as a crew of skeletons whose weird cries and howls often terrify the Chilote sailor. There are skilled "brujos," or wizards, on Chiloe who make a living in selling spells for warding off the doom set upon the native fishermen by the *Caleuche.* This phantom ship has been sighted as far South as the Horn and as far North as the Peruvian coast, though never very far from the land.

The place to hear stories of the *Caleuche* is in the shack of some mestizo or half-breed fisherman when the wind is roaring outside and the embers on the fire crackling within; then one hears all the old lore that has come down from father to son dealing with the sea, with ships, with fish and fowl and even monsters of the deep, but always the talk veers round at the last to the fiery *Flying Dutchman* of the Chilian coast.

The *Caleuche* has hardly ever been seen in the spring or summer, its appearance being usually confined to winter and late autumn. People ashore have reported the Chilote phantom ship sailing along the coast in a mist of fire or even high up in the sky surrounded by a greeny-blue sea of its own, which shows up against the black vault of heaven.

There is only one occasion on which the appearance of the *Caleuche* arouses no misgivings, and that is at Carelmapu on New Year's Eve. As soon as it is dark all the inhabitants gather on the shore, then clams are cooked on the ground and the fiery local spirit passed round. Thus the time until midnight is spent in eating and drinking and spinning yarns about the *Caleuche*. Then at the first sound of the midnight bells, the simple fisherfolk declare that the *Caleuche* rises out of the sea, its rigging showing like a silver web in the moonlight and its ancient out of date hull aglow clear-cut and distinct. Imagination no doubt adds much to the picture before which all hands bow their heads.

Returning to the missing *Kobenhavn*, the report of the coasters of Southern Chile was that during a furious norther in July, 1929, which raged along the whole length of Chile, a big dismasted sailing ship was seen opposite Chiloe with the dreaded *Caleuche*, all ablaze, following in its wake.

The reader may ask if others besides Chilotes have seen the *Caleuche*, which is most often reported in the Golfo de Penas, or Gulf of Sorrow, where the most terrific gales are met with.

Let me quote a letter from a seafaring correspondent:

> My own experience with the famous *Caleuche* dates back to 1905, when I was on board the P.S.N.Co.'s ss. *Chile* travelling to Corral. The captain came on board late in the evening. The barometer was falling and sky menacing. Got the anchor up about 8 p.m., and were struck by the first squalls about one hour out from Lota.
>
> It blew a whole gale for 36 hours and I never thought we should live through that wind and sea. I was on deck the whole night and only went into my cabin about one o'clock in the morning to change clothes, get my rubbers and cigarettes. The confusion below was terrible; and the smell, the water, and the cries of the passengers drove me on deck again just in time to see a big sea carry away one of the boats.
>
> In the early morning hours, when it was just bright enough to see, some sailors came along the boat deck to clear up the wreckage. Amongst these sailors were some natives from Chiloe, who insisted that the *Caleuche* had passed, ablaze and sailing dead against the wind, about 3 o'clock in the morning.
>
> My stand was amongst the coaling gear, just behind the funnel, where I found good shelter, and I could see well around me when on the crest of a wave, but I saw nothing beyond ink-black seas and the foam and spindrift which blew over the funnel at intervals.

When the mere sight of the blazing *Caleuche* spells almost certain death to the seer, it is not very surprising if the evidence is mostly hearsay, yet there is sufficient to convince anyone who has had any experience in psychic matters.

The Nitrate Ports.

Whilst Valparaiso was the chief port of entry to Chile, its export trade was quite insignificant compared to the nitrate ports such as Pisagua, Caleta Buena, Iquique, Tocopilla, Mejillones, Antofagasta, Taltal and Talcahuano.

The chief of these nitrate ports, Iquique, was a small

Peruvian fishing village in 1830 when the export of nitrate first began. This port, which right up to 1914 used often to be chock-a-block with big sailing ships, had a very rough time in its early days. In 1868 it was nearly destroyed by an earthquake; in 1875 it was gutted by fire; and two years later it was overwhelmed by earthquake, fire and tidal waves. It was first occupied by the Chilians in 1879 and was finally ceded to Chile by the treaty of October, 1883.

Pisagua Bay, to the northward, used to be a great place for boat sailing in the days of the windjammers. Most square-rig skippers prided themselves on being good boat sailors, and usually kept a smart gig in the davits specially for racing. This was often a ticklish business at Pisagua, as the wind coming off the high hills which surrounded the anchorage was usually very gusty with squalls of great violence.

However, apprentices were always very partial to Pisagua, for besides sailing races of a Saturday, Sundays were mostly spent on fishing excursions. Sporting skippers who were fishermen at heart would only allow a rod or hook and line to be used, but those whose only object was to obtain a boatful of fish were quite satisfied with the results caused by a stick of dynamite. These sticks of dynamite, with the necessary fuse and caps, could be bought, by the way, at any ship chandler's or grocer's store.

Caleta Buena, one of the smallest of the nitrate ports, is also one of the barest. It lies on the edge of a huge desert where nothing can grow, and from the sea the shore appears to be absolutely bleak and lifeless, with its yellow sun-scorched hills stretching right back to the distant snow peaks. At the anchorage, the nitrate traders sweep their spars backwards and forwards across the sky as they bow ceaselessly to the heave of the Pacific rollers.

Tocopilla, to the southward of Iquique, was another circular bay enclosed by a bluff at its northern end and a long reef of rocks at its southern end. The ships here lay in a single tier close in to the shore and stretched across from the reef to the bluff.

Almost all these nitrate ports had similar features: a more or less open roadstead, a precipitous rock face towering up behind the small town, and perhaps an isolated bluff or island at one or other end of the anchorage. Each place of course had its own difficulties. The anchorage at Mejillones was narrow and troublesome. Antofagasta had a dangerous bar, and one or two places were difficult to make, it being easy to drift by in the grip of the current, whilst the water was too deep to anchor in unless one could get close in to the shore.

Talcahuano—pronounced Turkey Warner by seamen—is one of the best harbours on the coast, being sheltered by the island of Quiriguina in Concepcion Bay. This in the old days used to be a great resort of the Nantucket and New Bedford whalers, which generally put in there to refit.

One or two of the nitrate ports, such as Chanaral, had no fresh water, every gallon having to be condensed from the sea. Such places recall memories of much weariness, rolling casks down to the landing place.

One of the barest spots was Junin Cove to the northward of Mejillones, which lies open to the south-easterly swell and affords no shelter or conveniences of any kind. Yet old sailormen nearly always preserve happy memories of the West Coast. Here is a clean-cut mind picture of Taltal by an

"PISAGUA" OFF DOVER

[*See page* 66

"PISAGUA" IN DOVER AFTER COLLISION

Photo by Amos & Amos, Dover

See page 66

"POTOSI." (OFF CAPE HORN, WESTWARD BOUND)

Lent by Captain George Schutze

[*See page* 70

old salt, taken from the Valparaiso paper, the *South Pacific Mail:*

> The sun is shining brightly on a number of sailing vessels moored in three tiers across an open bay, each with two anchors out ahead and one astern, lazily lifting and falling to the long Pacific swell. Between the tiers of ships, lighters, each sculled by two men with long sweeps over the stern, slowly make their way out with nitrate or return empty, while others, deeply laden with coal, are making their way shoreward, and ships' boats proceed on various errands.
>
> The slopes of the Andes descend steeply almost to the water's edge, and a cluster of whitewashed houses, gathered near a small iron mole in the centre of the bay, form the town of Taltal. Between the inside tier of ships and the beach lie several groups of general cargo lighters, awaiting the arrival of the mail boat, each guarded by a watchman and a dog, against predatory ships' apprentices or shore folk, for an apprentice is always ready to augment his scanty half-deck fare with a case of delicacies should he see any prospect of so doing, and some others are equally willing.
>
> The whole bay is edged with a line of white surf breaking on the shore and gleaming in the sunlight.

The photographs of Iquique and Pisagua give a very good idea of the great fleets of sailing ships which frequented the West Coast in the old days. What a change has been wrought on the Coast by time and machinery! The forests of masts have gone, and the graceful hulls no longer roll ceaselessly on the heavy mooring chains. Their place is filled by the great ugly ocean tramp, the abode of worry and hustle, with its everlasting clatter of winches.

PART II.—THE CLIPPERS.

ALTHOUGH there were more British sailing ships sailing to the West Coast of South America than vessels of any other nationality, none of our big shipping firms specialised in the nitrate trade like the German firm of Laeisz and the French firm of A. D. Bordes, nor did we reserve our fastest ships for the trade; in fact, in the early days the British West Coast traders were often the slowest sailers in the whole of our huge Mercantile Marine. Thus, when the nitrate clippers are spoken of, the reference is made to foreign and not British ships.

It was Herr F. Laeisz who really brought the spirit of hustle into the easy-going nitrate trade. He it was who required his captains to make racing passages. He it was who required his agents so to drive the West Coast stevedores that his ships were invariably discharged and loaded in a quarter of the time taken by those of any other firm and any other nationality.

Herr Laeisz also owed a great deal of his success in the nitrate trade to the wonderful lighterage organisation which he built up in the nitrate ports.

The "P" Line.

The great "P" Line of nitrate clippers started humbly at the beginning of the seventies with the 985-tonned iron full-rigged ship *Polynesia*, which was built at Hamburg in 1874. At about the same date Herr Laeisz bought a little iron barque of 537 tons, called the *Flottbeck*, which he renamed the *Professor*, and a wooden barque of 647 tons, called the *Henriette Vehn*, which seems to have been the only vessel belonging to Laeisz whose name did not begin with "P."

It was not until the end of the eighties that ships of any size were built for this famous Hamburg line, but several small barques were bought from British owners, such as the *Aminta*, which was renamed the *Pluto*; the *Weymouth*, renamed *Poncho*; the *Maggie Leslie*, renamed *Paquita*; and the *Peep o' Day*, renamed *Puck*.

The first ship to be built for Herr Laeisz by the famous firm of Blohm & Voss was the 1230-ton iron barque *Plus*, which was launched in 1885. Then came the steel barques, *Potrimpos*, 1273 tons, and the *Prompt*, 1445 tons, both launched in 1887. They were followed by the steel barque *Pamelia*, of 1442 tons, in 1888.

Herr Laeisz also bought three little 1000-ton iron barques built by Blohm & Voss. These were the *Pirat*, launched in 1883; *Pestalozzi*, launched in 1884; and *Paposo*, launched in 1885.

These comprised all the three-mast barques in the "P" Line fleet. They were followed at the end of the eighties by five magnificent steel ships, which registered a little over 1700 tons apiece. These were:

Palmyra	Built by	Blohm & Voss	at	Hamburg	in	1889
Parchim	,,	John C. Tecklenborg	,,	Geestemunde	,,	1889
Pera	,,	,, ,,	,,	,,	,,	1890
Pampa	,,	Act. Ges. Neptun	,,	Rostock	,,	1891
Preussen	,,	Blohm & Voss	,,	Hamburg	,,	1891

From the very first the "P" Line ships made a reputation for speed. For instance, the *Plus* made the following passages:

1894	Iquique to Hamburg	arr.	January 13	..	81 days
1897	,, St. Catherines	,,	November 30		77 ,,
1903	Dungeness to Valparaiso	,,	April 29	..	78 ,,

The little *Plus* was sold to Norway about five years before the War.

The *Pamelia* had a still finer record under the "P" Line house-flag. In 1902 she arrived at Valparaiso on February 7, only 65 days out from Dover. Her best round voyage was that of 1895, when she was commanded by H. A. Dehnhardt. Her passage from Hamburg to Valparaiso was made in 68 days, arriving on the day before Christmas, and the homeward passage, Iquique to Prawle Point, was made in the same time.

Pamelia made any number of passages under 80 days, both out and home. She was eventually sold, about the same time as the *Plus*, to Simonsen of Norway. Her sister ship, the *Prompt*, made the smartest outward passage to the West Coast in 1892, her time being 65 days from the Isle of Wight to Valparaiso. This ship was sold to the Finns about 1909.

"Pampa."

It would be hard to say which was the fastest of the "P" Line full-riggers; each one of them had a splendid list of good passages. As regards appearance they were worthy to be compared with the finest of the Clyde or Mersey beauties. I remember being so captivated by the majestic looks and seamanlike smartness of the *Pampa* as she lay in Antwerp spick and span amongst a dishevelled array of British, French, Norwegians and Dutch, that I went straight away and bought a photograph of her, which is illustrated here.

The *Pampa* was the only one of Laeisz's ships which was built at Rostock, and judging from her records I should say that she was quite as fast as any of the clippers built by either Blohm & Voss or Tecklenborg. She was rarely more than 80 days going out round the Horn and her homeward passages were equally good. The following are the best passages made by her in the first ten years of her life:

1892	Dungeness to Iquique	67 days
1893	Dungeness to Valparaiso	64 „
1893	Downs to Valparaiso	65 „
1894	Dungeness to Valparaiso	64 „
1895	Iquique to Prawle Point	75 „
1898	Iquique to Cuxhaven	69 „
1900	Dungeness to Valparaiso	73 „
1900	Iquique to Dungeness	70 „
1900	Caleta Buena to Cuxhaven	79 „
1901	Valparaiso to Dungeness	79 „
1903	Iquique to Isle of Wight	79 „

Captain Steincke commanded the *Pampa* until 1899, when he was succeeded by Captain Preutzmann. Then in 1902 Captain W. Schroder took over the *Pampa*, and commanded her until 1909, when Captain J. Hamm had her for a voyage or two. Her last commander under the "P" flag was Captain Jars, who had her until she was sold to the Finns in 1913.

The best passages accomplished by the *Pampa* between 1903 and 1913 were both made in 1905 under Captain Schroder:

Out	Elbe to Valparaiso	61 days
Home	Taltal to Isle of Wight	75 „

"Posen" ex "Preussen" I.

The first *Preussen*, which was renamed the *Posen* when the great five-master came out, seems to have had the next best record to the *Pampa* of Laeisz's full-riggers. Her best known commander was Captain B. R. Petersen, and the following are the pick of her passages to and from the West Coast:

1893	Start to Iquique	68 days
1895	Iquique to Dover	71 ,,
1896	Valparaiso to Hamburg	71 ,,
1898	Hamburg to Valparaiso	69 ,,
1898	Dover to Valparaiso	63 ,,
1900	Iquique to Isle of Wight	68 ,,
1900	Dover to Valparaiso	70 ,,
1900	Iquique to Prawle Point	68 ,,
1901	Dungeness to Valparaiso	75 ,,
1901	Iquique to Beachy Head	75 ,,
1902	Southampton to Iquique	72 ,,
1904	Elbe to Valparaiso	68 ,,
1905	Iquique to Scilly	81 ,,

In 1909, when outward bound to Valparaiso from Hamburg with gunpowder on board, this beautiful ship caught fire and blew up on October 14.

"Palmyra," "Parchim" and "Pera."

The records of these three ships are not quite so good as those of the two built in 1891, but there was probably very little difference in their sailing powers. The best passages made by *Palmyra* were as follows:

1895	Prawle Point to Valparaiso	67 days
1900	Lizard to Valparaiso	76 ,,
1903	Iquique to Prawle Point	77 ,,
1903	Dover to Valparaiso	66 ,,
1904	Scilly to Valparaiso	76 ,,

The following were the commanders of the *Palmyra*: Captain G. Schluter to 1897; Captain C. V. Jessen to 1903; Captain E. Paulsen to 1906; and Captain P. Petersen.

Whilst bound from Antwerp to Valparaiso with general cargo in 1908, *Palmyra* was wrecked on July 2 on Wellington Island.

The best of *Parchim's* records between her launch and the date of her sale to the Finns were:

1893	Iquique to Isle of Wight	72 days
1894	Cuxhaven to Iquique	74 ,,
1897	Iquique to Dungeness	72 ,,
1902	Taltal to Isle of Wight	75 ,,
1906	Iquique to Scilly	69 ,,
1908	Scilly to Taltal	73 ,,

This ship seems to have been constantly changing her captain, the following each sailing her for a few voyages:—C. Blose, H. Nissen, M. Grapow, F. Ahrens, A. Oetzmann, and H. A. Siemer. In 1912 she was bought by Captain Erikson; then in 1913 we find her crossing from Newcastle, N.S.W., to Valparaiso in 57 days, and then loading home from Mejillones. On this voyage she was commanded by the well-known Captain Lundquist, and I believe that M. Lundquist of Mariehamn was her chief owner.

The *Pera*, which also went to the Finns, being bought by M. Lundquist in 1910, made the following passages under Laeisz's house-flag:

1893	Dover to Valparaiso	74 days
1894	Iquique to Dover	81 ,,
1897	Hamburg to Talcahuano	72 ,,
1905	Taltal to Scilly	70 ,,
1907	Scilly to Valparaiso	68 ,,

Her best known commander was Captain A. Teschler, who sailed her for about ten years. He was succeeded in 1906 by Captain A. Alwardt.

"Placilla" and "Pisagua."

In 1892 John C. Tecklenborg built two magnificent four-mast barques for F. Laeisz. These were the *Placilla* and

"POTOSI"

Lent by Reederei F. Laeisz [*See page* 70

"PREUSSEN"

Lent by F. Laeisz [*See page* 86

"PREUSSEN"

[*See page* 86

the *Pisagua.* The former registered 2895 tons gross, 2780 nett; and the latter 2906 tons gross, 2763 nett.

Both these big four-masters made splendid passages in the nitrate trade. The *Placilla* was taken from the stocks by Captain Hilgendorf, who afterwards commanded the famous *Potosi.* On her maiden voyage she passed the Lizard on March 2, 1892, and arrived at Valparaiso on April 29, only 58 days out.

Other records worthy of note were:

1892	Iquique to Prawle Point	77 days
1893	Hamburg to Valparaiso	67 „
1893	Iquique to Lizard	70 „
1895	Pisagua to Lizard	77 „
1897	Beachy Head to Valparaiso	73 „
1897	Iquique to Dungeness	77 „
1899	Prawle Point to Iquique	60 „

For some reason or other F. Laeisz sold this fine ship to the Reederiakt. Ges. von 1896 of Hamburg in 1900, and she was afterwards renamed the *Optima.* She seems to have maintained her fine passages, however, as witness the following:

1901	Port Talbot to Caleta Buena	81 days
1901	Iquique to Dover	86 „
1902	Port Talbot to Iquique	70 „

Throughout her existence under her new owners she was commanded by Captain F. W. Thom, but her life as the *Optima* was a short one, for she was wrecked in January, 1905.

The *Pisagua* will be chiefly remembered for her disastrous collision with the P. & O. liner *Oceana* off Beachy Head in March, 1912. Launched in September, 1892, her first commander was C. Bahlke. Then H. Dehnhardt took her in 1902, and finally R. Dahm was in command.

The following are her best passages:

1892	Dover to Valparaiso	72 days
1893	Iquique to Prawle Point	75 ,,
1894	Lizard to Iquique	69 ,,
1894	Iquique to Dover	80 ,,
1895	Eastbourne to Iquique	72 ,,
1895	Iquique to Beachy Head	81 ,,
1895	Dover to Valparaiso	73 ,,
1899	Iquique to Prawle Point	78 ,,
1900	Iquique to Dover	77 ,,
1902	Beachy Head to Valparaiso	76 ,,
1902	Iquique to Isle of Wight	80 ,,
1903	Downs to Valparaiso	73 ,,
1903	Iquique to Prawle Point	76 ,,
1903	Isle of Wight to Valparaiso	73 ,,
1905	Iquique to Scilly	72 ,,
1910	Lizard to Talcahuano	65 ,,

The "Pisagua" - "Oceana" Collision.

At 4.30 a.m. on Saturday, March 16, 1912, the *Pisagua*, with nitrate from Mejillones, was beating up Channel under full sail, when she ran into the P. & O. liner *Oceana*, which was outward bound to Bombay. The collision occurred right in the track of the Newhaven-Dieppe cross-Channel boat, the *Pisagua* striking the liner almost at right angles on her port side nearly abreast of her foremast, and tearing two large holes in her hull.

At the first alarm there was something like a panic amongst the Lascar crew aboard the *Oceana*, but her officers and white crew soon restored order; lifebelts were served out, and the boats quickly lowered. Unfortunately the first boat was swamped, and seven passengers and several members of the crew drowned, the only person saved from her being a lady passenger, Miss Macfarlane, who clung to the keel of the boat until she was picked up by those in the second boat lowered.

Her father, Mr. J. L. Macfarlane, a Glasgow banker, was drowned.

This was the first occasion on which the Peninsular & Oriental Company lost a passenger by accident at sea.

Very shortly after the collision the Newhaven mail boat *Sussex* came up and took off twenty-seven passengers and most of the crew, the remainder being landed at Eastbournc by the Newhaven and Eastbourne lifeboats. Captain Hide, the pilot, and sixteen officers and men of the crew remained aboard, whilst the *Oceana* was taken in tow by the tug *Alert* and one of Rea's steamers. The liner was very much down at the head and it was found expedient to tow her stern first.

The idea was to beach her, but from the first it was evident that the ship might sink at any moment. After a short time Captain Hide realised that the condition of the *Oceana* was too critical for anyone to remain aboard of her, and he and his crew were thereupon transferred to the tug *Alert*. In spite of every effort the *Alert* was unable to get the *Oceana* into shoal water before she sank. This occurred at 10 a.m. in 12 fathoms of water, the ship's position being 6 miles S.E. of Eastbourne pier and 2 miles W. of the *Royal Sovereign*.

Meanwhile the *Pisagua*, with her bows stove in, her forepeak full of water, and her head gear and fore royal and topgallant masts and yards carried away, stood on to the eastward. Luckily the weather remained quiet, and with the aid of the tugs *Arcadia* and *Conqueror* she was able to reach an anchorage in Dover harbour by the afternoon of March 16.

On examination the damage to the bows of the *Pisagua* proved very extensive, and the ship would have gone down like a stone if the fore bulkhead had given. This, however, was shored up, and the additional precaution of keeping the Dover tugs standing by her was resorted to.

On March 23 the steamer *Magdelena Blumenthal* was moored alongside the *Pisagua*, and 2150 tons of the nitrate were transferred to the former's hold. The barque was then taken into the tidal basin and laid aground, so that she would dry at low water. Temporary repairs were then made to her bow, and at 1 p.m. on April 3 she left Dover for Hamburg in tow of the two German tugs *Roland* and *Simson* and arrived on April 6.

Meanwhile Captain Young and his divers had been busy salving specie from the *Oceana*, their efforts being much interfered with by stormy weather.

One hardly realises the amount of bullion travelling about the world in our great liners, but the following reports from the salvers of the *Oceana's* treasure give some idea of the romance of the diver's profession:

March 18.—Salvage Association report that, with the approval of the Peninsular & Oriental Company, arrangements have been made with the Liverpool Salvage Association for the recovery of the gold and silver on board the *Oceana*. In accordance with these arrangements the salvage steamer *Ranger*, with divers and equipments, was despatched from Holyhead on Saturday and is now due at the *Oceana*.

March 22.—Strong wind, sea rough, impossible to work.

March 23.—Weather fine, the *Ranger* proceeding to wreck immediately.

March 24.—Position of ship unchanged, but wind and sea increased at low water and prevented diving operations.

March 25.—Dense fog, strong sea, no work possible.

March 29.—Too much sea for divers to go down.

March 30.—Heavy sea at wreck. Impossible to work.

April 1.—Too much sea for working, tide very strong, wind N.E., moderate gale.

April 2.—Weather fine, proceeding to wreck.

April 4.—Went out early this morning, worked low water tide, recovered 10 boxes of specie. Hope to work again to-day at high water. At high water *Ranger* got into position, when strong wind arose, making work impossible.

April 6.—Work still impossible, too much sea.

April 7.—1.4 p.m. Recovered 6 boxes of gold, also 2 boxes of bar silver, and 2 ingots of silver from forward.

April 7.—6.50 p.m. Recovered 44 bars of silver this tide.

April 8.—Weather bad, no work possible.

April 9.—Divers salved 6 pieces of gold, and some silver, together worth £40,000. The weather afterwards became so bad that the *Ranger* was unable to land the specie.

April 11.—At low water wind and sea increased, making diving impossible.

April 12.—Saved 40 bars of silver. Divers had a great deal of debris to clear away from port forward hatch on hurricane deck, but eventually started hatchway.

April 13.—Recovered 88 bars of silver, and on evening tide 130 bars of silver.

April 14.—On morning tide recovered 111 bars of silver. On evening tide recovered 120 bars of silver.

April 15.—Strong sea, no work possible. It is now necessary to cut away a quantity of wire rigging in order to facilitate access to after specie room as the baskets now caught in the debris on their way up.

April 16.—Fresh easterly wind, too much sea to work.

April 18.—Recovered 120 bars of silver in the morning. The divers had little time to work owing to the strong tides.

April 19.—Morning recovered 106 bars of silver; afternoon tide, 107 bars of silver and 1 box of gold.

April 20.—Recovered 167 bars of silver.

April 21.—Recovered 236 bars of silver and 1 box of gold.

April 22.—Recovered 76 bars of silver and 1 box of gold.

By the end of April all the bullion had been salved, and the divers were at work recovering casks of ivory. At 2 a.m. on June 10 a large two-masted steamer fouled the wreck and bent the mainmast over to starboard, so that it could no longer be used for mooring to. By July 5, all the bullion and ivory having been recovered from the wreck, the *Oceana* was blown up in sections.

Meanwhile the *Pisagua*, after being repaired, was sold to the Norwegians, and on June 11 she left Hamburg under the command of Captain Larsen for Sandefjord. On October 17 she left Sandefjord for the South Shetlands loaded with coal and provisions for the floating refineries and whalers. Captain Larsen put into Leith on October 23, and did not sail again until November 8. Nothing more was heard until February 12, 1913, when a cable from Punta Arenas announced that the *Pisagua* had stranded on the South Shetlands not far from the whaling station and had become a total loss.

The Mighty "Potosi."

The next ship to be launched for Laeisz's "P" Line of nitrate clippers was the magnificent steel five-mast barque, *Potosi*, built by Tecklenborg at Geestemunde and launched July, 1895. Shipping people declared that Herr Laeisz built *Potosi* in order to rival the British-built French five-masted barque *France*. Both as regards her carrying capacity—which was over 6000 tons—and her sailing powers, the *Potosi*, it was hoped, would put the *France* entirely in the shade. In her construction she was specially stiffened and strengthened in order to support her great sail area without straining.

The *France*, which was built by Henderson at Partick for Messrs. A. D. Bordes, had made an outward passage in 1892 of 74 days from Dunkirk. The *Potosi* had no difficulty in beating this record on her maiden passage. Under the command of Captain Hilgendorf she took her departure from the Weser on July 26, 1895, and on August 1 was off Ushant. The Equator was crossed 20 days 8 hours out from Ushant, and on September 14 the *Potosi* crossed 50° S. in 64° W. when

24 days from the Equator. On the next day she rounded Cape St. John in the teeth of a westerly gale.

The best running on the passage was made on September 20 and 21, when the five-master covered 650 miles in 48 hours, with an easterly gale behind her. In one watch she sailed 66 miles, giving an average of 16·5 knots.

On October 6 she came to an anchor in Iquique Roads, 66 days from the Channel and 73 days from Germany.

In 1895 the "P" Line had not brought its discharging and loading organisation on the West Coast to the perfection which it afterwards reached. Nevertheless the *Potosi* was only twenty days discharging ballast and loading 6000 tons of saltpetre. She sailed from Iquique on October 26, and, passing in sight of the Diego Ramirez Rocks on the 21st day out, rounded the Horn on November 15.

In the South Atlantic the big ship was not favoured by the wind, and she took 29 days from the Horn to the Equator, which was crossed on December 14. This was made up for by an exceedingly good run of 18½ days from the Equator to the Lizard. During the last eight days of this traverse, from 27° N., 38° W., to the Lizard, the *Potosi* averaged 11 knots. The headland was sighted on January 2, 1896, the *Potosi* being then 68 days out from Iquique. Head winds were encountered in the Channel, and the new ship was five days beating up, until January 7, when a Dutch tug took hold of her abreast of the *Galloper* and towed her to Cuxhaven in 4 days, her total passage to Cuxhaven thus being 77 days, and her arrival date January 11.

Her first voyage proved that the *Potosi* was an excellent all-round boat, sailing well on all points and able to log over

16 knots in strong fair winds. On her first homeward passage she fell in with the smart little wool clipper *Cimba*, in the South Atlantic. The *Cimba* was off the Diego Ramirez at noon on November 12, and on the 27th she was overhauled by the *Potosi*. For the next three days the two vessels kept within sight of each other, *Cimba's* runs being 88, 205 and 211. Then the *Potosi* seems to have got clean away from her, as *Cimba* did not cross the Equator until December 18, and on the last leg of the passage dropped still further behind, only signalling the Lizard on January 17, 15 days after the *Potosi* had passed up.

Compared with the *Potosi* the *Cimba* was, of course, a tiny little ship, as she only registered 1174 tons, but she had made quite a reputation as a wool clipper. The two vessels met again when outward bound in 1902. The following entries from *Cimba's* log show that in the strong head winds *Potosi* still had the best of it:

October 17.—Lat. 6° 58′ N., long. 21° 31′ W. Course S. 60° E. Dist. 146 miles. Wind south, strong and squally. *Potosi* 7 miles to windward.
October 24.—Lat. 2° 31′ N., long. 21° 10′ W. Course S. 58° W. Dist. 130 miles. Wind south, moderate and cloudy. *Potosi* 7 miles to leeward.
October 25.—Lat. 1° 20′ N., long. 23° 34′ W. Course S. 64° W. Dist. 161 miles. Wind S. by E. *Potosi* at noon 5 miles ahead; at dark nearly out of sight ahead.

A writer in *The Field* a few years ago, discussing the speed of large sailing vessels, gives the following delightful word picture of *Potosi* under sail:

I was fortunate in seeing the *Potosi* on an occasion when she furnished the finest action picture which I have ever seen.

It was blowing a moderate gale, and the vessel I was in had nothing set above upper topsails, when a white cloud of canvas was sighted ahead, which quickly developed into the *Potosi*, bound the other way under full sail.

In justice to ourselves I must say that we were close-hauled, whilst she had the wind two points abaft the beam. She passed close to windward of us carrying

"PREUSSEN"
Wrecked off Dover; after Collision

Topical Press Photo [*See page* 95

"PREUSSEN"
Wrecked off Dover

Topical Press Photo [*See page* 95

"PAMIR"

Lent by Nautical Photo Agency [*See page* 100

"PASSAT"

Lent by Reederei F. Laeisz [*See page* 103

42 sails, 24 square and 18 fore-and-afters. She was lying well over, her lee scuppers were awash, and at times, as she rolled slightly, even her lee rail seemed to be near the water as she tore along in a smother of foam.

I was to meet her again two years later under circumstances which brought out not only her speed but the daring and skilful manner in which she was navigated. At the time I was a junior officer in a 12-knot steamer bound for Hamburg. At the entrance to the English Channel about noon we sighted a five-masted barque standing in towards the Lizard to signal. It was the *Potosi* from Iquique, also bound for Hamburg. The wind was from the south-west, freshening, with driving rain squalls, and she was soon blotted out from view by one of them.

We did not sight her again, but I pictured the great lofty vessel storming her way up Channel and through the Narrows in the murk and gloom, with all sail set, for I knew that she was driven as hard as any of the old packet ships. I was not, however, quite prepared for what followed.

Steaming 12 knots all the way, we picked up our pilot at 2 p.m. on the second day after we had sighted the *Potosi*. As we stood in towards the mouth of the river our captain said: "We sighted the *Potosi* off the Lizard, pilot. There has been a fair wind ever since, and she ought to be along to-night."

The pilot smiled, a rather cynical smile, I thought.

"The *Potosi* passed in this morning, captain," he said.

The following is a complete epitome of *Potosi's* voyages under the "P" Line house-flag:

SECOND VOYAGE.

Commander—Captain Hilgendorf.

March 8, 1896	Left Cuxhaven			
	Cuxhaven to Lizard	6	days	
	Lizard to Equator	20	,,	
	Equator to Cape Horn	28	,,	
	C. Horn to Caleta Buena	17	,,	
May 18, 1896	Arrived Caleta Buena	65	,,	from Lizard
		71	,,	from Cuxhaven
June 2, 1896	Left Caleta Buena			
	Caleta Buena to C. Horn	24	days	
	Cape Horn to Equator	26	,,	
	Equator to Lizard	28	,,	
	Caleta Buena to Lizard	78	,,	
	Lizard to Hamburg	4	,,	
August 23, 1896	Arrived Cuxhaven	82	,,	from Caleta Buena

THIRD VOYAGE.

Commander—Captain Hilgendorf.

November 12, 1896	Left Cuxhaven		
	Cuxhaven to Lizard	5 days	
	Lizard to Equator	23 ,,	
	Equator to Cape Horn	23 ,,	
	Cape Horn to Valparaiso	13 ,,	
January 15, 1897	Arrived Valparaiso	59 ,,	from Lizard
		64 ,,	from Cuxhaven

This was the best outward passage of the year.

February 16, 1897	Left Iquique		
	Iquique to Cape Horn	22 days	
	Cape Horn to Equator	26 ,,	
	Equator to Cuxhaven	36 ,,	
May 11, 1897	Arrived Cuxhaven	84 ,,	out

Goffey's *Micronesia*, a 1500-ton iron full-rigger with a very nice turn of speed, being also homeward bound from Iquique with nitrate, was three days in company with the *Potosi* on this passage, after which, however, she was dropped steadily astern.

FOURTH VOYAGE.

Commander—Captain Hilgendorf.

July 23, 1897	Passed Isle of Wight	
October 1, 1897	Arrived Valparaiso	70 days from the Wight
November 5, 1897	Left Iquique	
January 21, 1898	Passed Dungeness	77 days out

FIFTH VOYAGE.

Commander—Captain Hilgendorf.

May 14, 1898	Passed Isle of Wight	
July 15, 1898	Arrived Valparaiso	62 days from the Wight

Best passage of the year.

August 18, 1898	Left Caleta Buena	
October 31, 1898	Arrived Cuxhaven	74 days out

SIXTH VOYAGE.

Commander—Captain Hilgendorf.

December 20, 1898	Passed Portland	
February 20, 1899	Arrived Iquique	62 days from the Wight
March 7, 1899	Left Iquique	
May 20, 1899	Passed Prawle Point	74 days out

SEVENTH VOYAGE.

Commander—Captain Hilgendorf.

July 11, 1899	Passed Beachy Head	
September 17, 1899	Arrived Iquique	68 days from Beachy Hd.
October 6, 1899	Left Caleta Buena	
December 15, 1899	Passed Isle of Wight	70 days out

Best passage of the year.

EIGHTH VOYAGE.

Commander—Captain Hilgendorf.

March 15, 1900	Left Hamburg	
March 17, 1900	Put to sea from the Elbe	
March 20, 1900	Off Dover	
March 21, 1900	Passed the Isle of Wight	
April 3, 1900	In 10° N., 26° W.	
May 15, 1900	Arrived Valparaiso	55 days out from I.O.W.
May 23, 1900	Arrived Iquique	

On the way up the Coast from the Horn the following splendid runs were made:

May 10	.. 278 miles	May 13	.. 345 miles
May 11	.. 378 „	May 14	.. 283 „
May 12	.. 322 „		

giving a total of 1045 miles in three days and 1606 miles in five days.

June 7, 1900	Left Iquique	
August 19, 1900	Passed the Lizard	73 days out
August 23, 1900	Arrived Cuxhaven	
August 26, 1900	Arrived Hamburg	

NINTH VOYAGE.

Commander—Captain Hilgendorf.

September 18, 1900	Left Hamburg with 2500 tons of sand ballast	
September 25, 1900	Passed Ushant	
December 5, 1900	Arrived Iquique	61 days from Ushant

Discharging of ballast had to be done by the crew and there was no donkey engine aboard to help them. After 11 days' strenuous work Messrs. Weber & Co. despatched the *Potosi* on her homeward passage. Mr. A. Groothoff, F. Laeisz's agent, was chiefly responsible for this smart piece of work.

December 16, 1900	Left Iquique	
February 27, 1901	Passed the Lizard	73 days out
March 2, 1901	Arrived Cuxhaven	
March 6, 1901	Berthed at Hamburg	

Great efforts were made to discharge the 6100 tons of nitrate by March 13, so as to accomplish the wonderful performance of two complete voyages between March 14, 1900, and March 14, 1901.

TENTH VOYAGE.

Commander—Captain Hilgendorf.

May 1, 1901	Passed Beachy Head	
July 3, 1901	Arrived Valparaiso	63 days from Beachy Hd.
August 15, 1901	Left Iquique	
November 2, 1901	Passed Prawle Point	79 days out

ELEVENTH VOYAGE.

Commander—Captain Schluter.

January 29, 1902	Passed the Lizard	
April 25, 1902	Arrived Valparaiso	86 days from the Lizard
June 8, 1902	Left Iquique	
August 23, 1902	Passed Prawle Point	76 days out

TWELFTH VOYAGE.

Commander—Captain Schluter.

September 24, 1902	Passed Prawle Point	
December 11, 1902	Arrived Tocopilla	78 days from Prawle Point
December 25, 1902	Left Caleta Buena	
March 12, 1903	Passed the Isle of Wight	77 days out

THIRTEENTH VOYAGE.

Commander—Captain H. Nissen.

April 14, 1903	Passed Prawle Point	
June 21, 1903	Arrived Iquique	68 days from Prawle Point
July 5, 1903	Left Iquique	
August 31, 1903	Passed Prawle Point	57 days out
September 4, 1903	Arrived mouth of the Elbe	
September 7, 1903	Arrived Hamburg	

FOURTEENTH VOYAGE.

Commander—Captain H. Nissen.

November 4, 1903	Passed the Isle of Wight	
January 11, 1904	Arrived Valparaiso	68 days from I.O.W.
February 12, 1904	Left Caleta Buena	
April 26, 1904	Passed Prawle Point	74 days out

FIFTEENTH VOYAGE.

Commander—Captain H. Nissen.

May 23, 1904	Passed Isle of Wight	
August 2, 1904	Arrived Iquique	71 days from I.O.W.
August 13, 1904	Left Iquique	
November 7, 1904	Passed Lizard	86 days out

SIXTEENTH VOYAGE.

Commander—Captain H. Nissen.

January 15, 1905	Left Hamburg	
January 20, 1905	Passed Isle of Wight	
February 7, 1905	Crossed the Equator	
March 6, 1905	Off Cape Horn	
March 20, 1905	Arrived Valparaiso	59 days from I.O.W.
May 12, 1905	Left Caleta Buena	
August 5, 1905	Passed Dover	85 days out

SEVENTEENTH VOYAGE.

Commander—Captain H. Nissen.

September 22, 1905	Passed Dover	
December 5, 1905	Arrived Valparaiso	74 days from Dover
January 25, 1906	Left Iquique	
April 21, 1906	Passed Prawle Point	86 days out

EIGHTEENTH VOYAGE.

Commander—Captain H. Nissen.

June 17, 1906	Passed Isle of Wight	
August 21, 1906	Arrived Valparaiso	65 days from I.O.W.
December 6, 1906	Left Iquique	
February 20, 1907	Passed Dover	76 days out

NINETEENTH VOYAGE.

Commander—Captain H. Nissen.

June 3, 1907	Passed Isle of Wight	
August 20, 1907	Arrived Valparaiso	78 days from I.O.W.
November 24, 1907	Left Iquique	
February 19, 1908	Passed Isle of Wight	87 days out

TWENTIETH VOYAGE.

Commander—Captain H. Nissen.

July 4, 1908	Passed Dover	
September 21, 1908	Arrived Coquimbo	79 days from Dover
October 28, 1908	Left Tocopilla (6000 tons of saltpetre on a draught of 25 ft.)	
November 12, 1908	Off Cape Horn	
December 7, 1908	Crossed the Line	
December 23, 1908	Off the Lizard	56 days out
January 2, 1909	Arrived Hamburg	

On the last eleven days of the passage before making her number off the Lizard the *Potosi* made the following sailing record:

December 13	.. 226 miles	December 19	.. 337 miles
„ 14	.. 232 „	„ 20	.. 279 „
„ 15	.. 248 „	„ 21	.. 327 „
„ 16	.. 244 „	„ 22	.. 293 „
„ 17	.. 227 „	„ 23	.. 253 „
„ 18	.. 291 „		

amounting to 2957 miles.

This was Captain Nissen's last voyage, and he handed over the big ship to Captain Fromcke on arrival at Hamburg.

TWENTY-FIRST VOYAGE.

Commander—Captain Fromcke.

April 24, 1909	Left Cuxhaven		
	Cuxhaven to Lizard	7 days	
	Lizard to Equator	19 „	
	Equator to Cape Horn	27 „	
	Cape Horn to Taltal	16 „	
July 2, 1909	Arrived Taltal	62 „	from Lizard
July 17, 1909	Left Taltal		
	Taltal to Cape Horn	20 days	
	Cape Horn to Equator	19 „	
	Equator to Lizard	23 „	
	Lizard to Hamburg	9 „	
September 26, 1909	Arrived Cuxhaven	62 „	to Lizard

TWENTY-SECOND VOYAGE.

Commander—Captain Fromcke.

December 14, 1909	Left Cuxhaven		
	Cuxhaven to Lizard	5 days	
	Lizard to Equator	26 ,,	
	Equator to Cape Horn	25 ,,	
	Cape Horn to Valparaiso	16 ,,	
February 24, 1910	Arrived Valparaiso	67 ,,	from Lizard
April 3, 1910	Left Taltal		
	Taltal to Cape Horn	15 days	
	Cape Horn to Equator	31 ,,	
	Equator to Cuxhaven	39 ,,	
June 27, 1910	Arrived Cuxhaven	85 ,,	out

TWENTY-THIRD VOYAGE.

Commander—Captain Fromcke.

August 21, 1910	Left Cuxhaven		
	Cuxhaven to Lizard	5 days	
	Lizard to Equator	29 ,,	
	Equator to Cape Horn	23 ,,	
	Cape Horn to Talcahuano	11 ,,	
October 26, 1910	Arrived Talcahuano	61 ,,	from Lizard
November 26, 1910	Left Tocopilla		
	Tocopilla to Cape Horn	20 days	
	Cape Horn to Equator	23 ,,	
	Equator to Cuxhaven	33 ,,	
February 10, 1911	Arrived Cuxhaven	76 ,,	out

TWENTY-FOURTH VOYAGE.

Commander—Captain Fromcke.

June 26, 1911	Left Cuxhaven		
	Cuxhaven to Lizard	9 days	
	Lizard to Equator	29 ,,	
	Equator to Cape Horn	27 ,,	
	Cape Horn to Talcahuano	13 ,,	
September 11, 1911	Arrived Talcahuano	69 ,,	from Lizard

"PARMA"

Lent by the Nautical Photo Agency [*See page* 108

"PINNAS"

Lent by the Nautical Photo Agency [*See page* 108

"VILLE DU HAVRE"

[*See page* 116

"VILLE DU HAVRE"

[*See page* 116

October 20, 1911	Left Caleta Buena		
	Caleta Buena to C. Horn	28 days	
	Cape Horn to Equator	30 ,,	
	Equator to Lizard	29 ,,	
	Lizard to Cuxhaven	9 ,,	
January 24, 1912	Arrived Cuxhaven	87 ,,	to Lizard

TWENTY-FIFTH VOYAGE.

Commander—Captain Niethe.

March 31, 1912	Left Cuxhaven		
	Cuxhaven to Lizard	8 days	
	Lizard to Equator	19 ,,	
	Equator to Cape Horn	33 ,,	
	Cape Horn to Valparaiso	15 ,,	
June 14, 1912	Arrived Valparaiso	67 ,,	from Lizard
July 28, 1912	Left Mejillones		
	Mejillones to Cape Horn	26 days	
	Cape Horn to Equator	24 ,,	
	Equator to Lizard	30 ,,	
	Lizard to Cuxhaven	3 ,,	
October 19, 1912	Arrived Cuxhaven	80 ,,	to Lizard
		83 ,,	to Cuxhaven

TWENTY-SIXTH VOYAGE.

Commander—Captain Niethe.

January 4, 1913	Left Hamburg	
January 30, 1913	Spoken 19° N., 22° W.	
March 29, 1913	Arrived Valparaiso	84 days out
May 21, 1913	Left Mejillones	
July 13, 1913	Spoken 10° N., 27° W.	
August 17, 1913	In the Downs	88 days out
August 21, 1913	Arrived Hamburg	92 ,, out

In entering port was in collision with a lighter: latter damaged.

TWENTY-SEVENTH VOYAGE.

Commander—Captain ——

October 3, 1913	Left Hamburg	
October 9, 1913	Off the Lizard	
November 7, 1913	Crossed Equator	
December 3, 1913	Off Cape Horn	
December 17, 1913	Arrived Valparaiso	69 days from Lizard
January 30, 1914	Left Iquique	
March 19, 1914	In 1° S., 25° W.	
April 17, 1914	Arrived Falmouth	
April 25, 1914	Arrived Hamburg	77 days to Falmouth

TWENTY-EIGHTH VOYAGE.

Last Passage under German Flag.

Commander—Captain ——

July 4, 1914	Left Hamburg	
July 11, 1914	Off the Lizard	
August 11, 1914	Crossed the Equator	
September 5, 1914	Off Cape Horn	
September 23, 1914	Arrived Valparaiso	74 days from Lizard

Throughout the war *Potosi* sheltered at Valparaiso. At various times it was reported that she was being fitted with auxiliary engines, and it was at one time confidently expected that she would put to sea as a raider.

In 1918 Herr Laeisz sold her to Vinnen, but she had to be surrendered to France under the terms of peace.

During her enforced inactivity the *Potosi* suffered severely, and before handing her over her crew took care to wreck her steering gear and so damaged her aloft that it was found necessary to renew nearly all the standing and running rigging before she could be sent to sea.

The Chilians, who had taken possession of the *Potosi*

some time before the Armistice, handed her over to France as soon as the terms of the Treaty of Versailles were known. The French, however, did nothing with the big ship, and at last, in 1923, the *Potosi* was taken over by Gonzales Soffia & Co. of Valparaiso, and a year later sailed for Hamburg with a cargo of nitrate under the name of *Flora.* On March 24, 1925, the great five-master passed Dungeness, arriving Hamburg on the 30th, 110 days out.

On her last voyage the *Flora* ex *Potosi* loaded 5000 tons of patent fuel and 800 tons of coal and coke at Cardiff, which port was left on July 13 for Mejillones. Nothing more was heard of the *Flora* for a couple of months, and then the underwriters received a most alarming cable from Buenos Aires stating that on September 16 an Argentine steamer had spoken her in 45° S., 66° W., and that she was on fire and heading in for the land to the North-West. Then on September 18 she anchored at Comodoro Rivadavia in the Gulf of St. George, being still on fire. Pumps from the Government oil fields were hurriedly brought down to the ship, and it was hoped that the fire would be extinguished, or at any rate got under control, by means of steam injected below. However, in spite of frenzied work with these steam pumps the fire continued to spread, and on October 1 two explosions occurred and the mainmast went over the side.

Realising that his vessel was doomed, the captain now made an attempt to beach her. This plan, however, had to be abandoned owing to the fierceness of the fire, which compelled the crew to leave her.

The next news received by the underwriters was a cable to the effect that the *Flora* was drifting about 25 miles South of

Comodoro Rivadavia, and was a danger to navigation. The end of Herr Laeisz's famous nitrate clipper was brought about by an Argentine cruiser, which sank her by shell fire. Nothing was saved except three lifeboats and a few odds and ends of gear.

Just about the time that the *Potosi* was going to her death the shipping press started an argument with regard to the sailing qualities of the "P" Line and other five-masters. One or two people declared that the *Potosi* was by no means a flyer, her maximum speed being 17 knots, and that her huge sail area and great length could not help but give her a good average in strong, fair winds. When close-hauled, they contended, she was by no means at her best. Other shipping experts gave the credit of her fine passages to her officers and crew. Under the "P" Line these consisted of:—Captain, three officers, two bosuns, sailmaker, carpenter, blacksmith, cook and steward, three or more apprentices, sixteen A.B.'s, and fourteen O.S.'s. Captain Johanne Fromcke considered that this was by no means a large crew for a vessel of the *Potosi*'s tonnage and sail area, and he declared that the *Potosi* owed her speed entirely to two factors: (1) The clever way in which her hull was designed; (2) the strength of her gear aloft.

The illustration of the *Potosi* close-hauled off the Horn in a hard gale of wind and carrying her lower topgallant sails on all four masts, proves the extraordinary power not only of the great ship herself but of her masts, spars and rigging. The strains must have been terrific, and her officers needed to keep a very sharp lookout upon the vast web of hemp, chain and steel which controlled the great area of canvas spread by the *Potosi's* five steel masts, of which the highest, the mainmast, measured 210 feet from deck to truck.

"Pitlochry" and "Persimmon."

In *Pitlochry* and *Persimmon* Herr Laeisz owned two of the finest four-mast barques which ever came out of a British yard. *Pitlochry* was built for the "P" Line by Stephen of Dundee and launched in September, 1894. Her first command was Captain G. Schluter, and he was followed in turn by Captains C. Gessen, J. Schmidt, R. Miethe, and H. Horn.

The following passages are an example of her sailing powers:

1897	Pisagua to St Catherine's	76 days
1900	Taltal to Prawle Point	79 „
1901	Dover to Valparaiso	77 „
1901-2	Hamburg to Taltal	65 „
1902	Caleta Buena to Prawle Pt.	77 „
1902	Hamburg to Valparaiso	69 „
1903	Iquique to Isle of Wight	75 „

The *Persimmon* was bought from the "Drum" Line in 1899. She was the *Drumrock*, the last of the "Drums," and one of the finest examples of Ramage & Ferguson's work. Besides being an excellent sailer she was most beautifully finished and elaborately fitted, possessing such unheard of luxuries as bathrooms for the crew.

Her first commander in the "P" Line was Captain H. A. Dehnhardt; then came H. Horn and E. Oetzmann. Here are a few of her passages in the nitrate trade:

1899	Ushant to Taltal	73 days
1899	Iquique to Prawle Point	79 „
1900	Dungeness to Taltal	76 „
1901	Dover to Valparaiso	71 „
1901	Iquique to Dungeness	87 „
1903	Dungeness to Valparaiso	75 „
1903	Iquique to Scilly	80 „

The *Persimmon* ended her days under the Canadian flag.

In 1925 she was cut down to a barge at Vancouver. She was then towed to and fro carrying logs from Queen Charlotte Island to the mills on the mainland. In 1927, whilst in tow of the *Pacific Monarch*, she stranded on the rocks in Queen Charlotte Sound and became a total loss.

"Preussen"—Five-mast Ship, "The Pride of Prussia."

In 1902 Tecklenborg built for Herr Laeisz the only five-masted sailing ship square-rigged on all five masts that was ever built. This was the mighty *Preussen.*

Preussen was a worthy rival of *Potosi.* Though the five-masted barque had the better of the five-masted ship in the matter of sailing records, there was very little to choose between them in actual speed through the water. Perfectly built, perfectly rigged, and perfectly run, Herr Laeisz, Tecklenborg, their captains and crews were rightly proud of these two great sailing ships, which were acknowledged by all sailormen to be the finest vessels relying on sail power only in the world.

The *Preussen* displaced 11,150 tons, her registered measurements at Lloyd's being: Gross 5081 tons, net 4788 tons. Her cargo capacity was reckoned at 8000 tons, and she carried 550 tons of water ballast. Her dimensions were as follows:

Length overall	433 feet	(133·5 metres)
Length registered	407·8 „	
Breadth, extreme	53·6 „	(16·4 metres)
Depth	27·1 „	(10 25 „)
Depth, moulded	32·6 „	
Draught loaded	8·23 metres	

Her sail area came out at 59,000 square feet, or 5560 quadrametres, and she spread forty-eight sails in all. Her highest mast, the middle mast, measured 68 metres from keel to truck. Her lower yards were 102 feet long (31·2 metres), with a diameter of 640 m.m. The royal yards measured 16 metres.

The following are a few items in her rigging outfit:

10,800 metres of standing rigging
13,230 metres of wire running rigging
17,260 metres of hemp running rigging
700 metres of chains
45 kilometres of towing hawsers
248 rigging screws
1260 blocks
560 metres of cable (of 65 m.m. strength and 66 tons weight)
6 anchors (the heaviest weighing 4000 k.g.)

All masts, yards, and spars were of steel. Instead of parrels for the yards, shoes of cast steel slid on rivetted iron bands. The standing rigging was all of Westphalian steel wire, the running rigging being either flexible wire or hemp. Halliards and braces all led through blocks to main deck capstans. Besides two steam pumps and two steam boilers in the deck-house, an engine drove four winches, the anchor capstan, and the steering apparatus. Abreast of the middle mast she had a midship bridge deck 93 feet long. Her topgallant foc's'le was 35 feet long and her poop 31 feet.

In her construction the *Preussen* was specially strengthened in many ways. For instance, transversal steadiness was obtained by beams in the hold made of half-box, which were tied together by heavy stringers. The deck beams, cross-pieces, and frames were made out of U-steel, and keelsons and side stringers were made to connect with intercostal plates which were rivetted to the ship's side making a particularly strong framework. Built up behind each of the five masts were stiffening supports, which were intended to take the main drag of the rigging from the ship's side.

Captain B. R. Petersen commanded the *Preussen* from her launch until April, 1909. Then Captain H. Nissen had her until she was wrecked.

The following is a complete record of her voyages:

MAIDEN VOYAGE.

July 31, 1902	Left Geestemunde	
August 4, 1902	Off Start Point	
	Spoken in 21° S., 39° W., when only 31 days out	
October 8, 1902	Arrived Iquique, 65 days from Start Point	
October 24, 1902	Left Iquique	
January 11, 1903	Off Scilly	79 days out
January 20, 1903	Arrived Cuxhaven	88 „ out

SECOND VOYAGE.

February 16, 1903	Left Hamburg	
March 5, 1903	Off Ushant	
March 18, 1903	Crossed Equator 13 days 8 hours from Ushant (a record)	
April 19, 1903	Crossed 50° S. (Atlantic)	23 days from the Line

Off the Horn had severe westerly and south-westerly gales.

April 21, 1903	Crossed 50° S. (Pacific)	11 days from 50° to 50°
May 1, 1903	Anchored Iquique	57 „ from Ushant
		74 „ „ Hamburg

Her fastest sailing was done on the port tack running up the South American coast. From noon April 23 to noon April 24 *Preussen* ran 368 miles by observation. From 4 to 8 a.m. on April 24 she logged 67 miles, and the log constantly registered 17 knots.

May 14, 1903	Left Iquique	
July 21, 1903	Off the Lizard	68 days out
July 25, 1903	Arrived Cuxhaven	72 „ out

"PACIFIQUE" EX "KNIGHT OF ST. MICHAEL"

[*See page* 122

"MADELEINE."

Lent by J. Randall

[*See page* 127

"JACQUELINE"
After Collision with a Cornish Headland

[*See page* 130

"RHONE"

[*See page* 130

THIRD VOYAGE.

August 20, 1903	Left Hamburg	
August 26, 1903	Off Scilly	
6th November, 1903	Arrived Tocopilla	72 days from Scilly
November 19, 1903	Left Tocopilla	
February 1, 1904	Off the Lizard	74 days out
February 4, 1904	Arrived Cuxhaven	77 ,, out

FOURTH VOYAGE.

March 10, 1904	Left Hamburg	
May 5, 1904	Arrived Tocopilla	65 days out
		62 ,, from Lizard
May 18, 1904	Left Tocopilla	
August 12, 1904	Arrived Hamburg	86 days out
		(80 days from Tocopilla to Channel)

FIFTH VOYAGE.

September 6, 1904	Left Hamburg	
November 12, 1904	Arrived Iquique	67 days out
		62 ,, from Lizard

On the run up the coast after rounding the Horn the *Preussen* covered 1008 miles in three days, and 1279 miles in four days, her week's run being:

November	3	271 miles	November	7	266 miles
,	4	328 ,,	,,	8	246 ,,
,,	5	347 ,,	,,	9	294 ,,
,,	6	333 ,,			

November 22, 1904	Left Iquique	
February 4, 1905	Arrived Hamburg	74 days out
		(69 days from Iquique to Channel)

SIXTH VOYAGE.

February 26, 1905	Left the Elbe	
March 4, 1905	Passed the Lizard	
March 25, 1905	Crossed the Line	21 days from the Lizard
April 25, 1905	Off Cape Horn	31 ,, from the Equator
May 22, 1905	Arrived Iquique	79 ,, out
May 31, 1905	Left Iquique	
July 17, 1905	In 6° N., 28° W.	
August 17, 1905	Off the Lizard	78 days out
August 21, 1905	Arrived Hamburg	82 ,, out

SEVENTH VOYAGE.

September 12, 1905	Left the Elbe	
September 16, 1905	Passed the Lizard	
October 13, 1905	Crossed the Line	
November 3, 1905	Off Cape Horn	
November 22, 1905	Arrived Iquique	67 days from the Lizard
December 1, 1905	Left Iquique	
December 20, 1905	Off Cape Horn	
January 18, 1906	Crossed the Line	
February 10, 1906	Off the Lizard	71 days from Iquique
February 13, 1906	Arrived Hamburg	74 ,, ,,

EIGHTH VOYAGE.

March 19, 1906	Left the Elbe	
March 21, 1906	Off the Lizard	
April 8, 1906	Crossed the Line	
May 13, 1906	Off Cape Horn	
May 29, 1906	Arrived Taltal	69 days from the Lizard
June 11, 1906	Left Taltal	
June 27, 1906	Off Cape Horn	
July 18, 1906	Crossed the Line	
August 22, 1906	Off the Lizard	
August 26, 1906	Arrived Hamburg	73 days to Lizard 77 ,, to Hamburg

NINTH VOYAGE.

September 20, 1906	Left the Elbe	
September 23, 1906	Off the Lizard	
October 19, 1906	Crossed the Line	
November 13, 1906	Off Cape Horn	
December 1, 1906	Arrived Taltal	69 days from Lizard
December 16, 1906	Left Taltal	
January 3, 1907	Off Cape Horn	
January 24, 1907	Crossed the Line	
February 16, 1907	Off the Lizard	
February 19, 1907	Arrived Hamburg	62 days to Lizard
		65 „ to Hamburg

TENTH VOYAGE.

May 5, 1907	Left Cuxhaven	
	Cuxhaven to Lizard	4 days
	Lizard to Equator	28 „
	Equator to Cape Horn	29 „
	Cape Horn to Valparaiso	23 „
July 28, 1907	Arrived Valparaiso	80 „ from Lizard
November 5, 1907	Left Tocopilla	
	Tocopilla to Cape Horn	18 days
	Cape Horn to Equator	20 „
	Equator to Lizard	24 „
	Lizard to Cuxhaven	5 „
January 11, 1908	Arrived Cuxhaven	67 „ out
		62 „ to Lizard

In the spring of 1908 Herr Laeisz was persuaded to charter the *Preussen* to the Standard Oil Company by Funch, Edye & Co. in order to take a cargo of oil out to Japan. The *Preussen* therefore left Cuxhaven on March 11, 1908, and arrived at New York on April 13, 33 days out.

The dates of her passage out to Yokohama were as follows:

May 27	Left New York	
July 1	Off Rio	
July 17	Crossed Cape Meridian	
August 8	In Lombok Strait	73 days out
August 16	Passed through Strait of Macassar	
August 25	Passed the Pelew Islands	
September 16	Arrived Yokohama	112 days out

This was a magnificent performance for a full built modern steel ship. The *Preussen* had a good chance of showing what she could do in strong, fair winds when running her easting down between Tristan da Cunha and Lombok Strait. In 11 days she covered 3019 miles, her 24-hour runs being:

July	21	300	July	27	232
„	22	308	„	28	341
„	23	310	„	29	323
„	24	249	„	30	236
„	25	218	„	31	255
„	26	247			

After spending a month at Yokohama, where she was greatly admired, the *Preussen* sailed on October 16 for the West Coast, and arrived at Taltal on December 30. She left Taltal on January 13, 1909, in order to complete her loading at Tocopilla. Tocopilla was reached on January 15, and on the 20th the *Preussen* sailed for Hamburg. Her times between points on this passage were as follows:

	Tocopilla to Cape Horn	21 days	
	Cape Horn to Equator	22 „	
	Equator to Lizard	26 „	
	Lizard to Hamburg	6 „	
April 5, 1909	Arrived Cuxhaven	75 „	out

TWELFTH VOYAGE.

May 6, 1909	Left Cuxhaven			
	Cuxhaven to Lizard	5	days	
	Lizard to Equator	22	,,	
	Equator to Cape Horn	33	,,	
	Cape Horn to Taltal	19	,,	
July 26	Arrived Taltal	74	,,	from Lizard
August 24, 1909	Left Tocopilla			
	Tocopilla to Cape Horn	25	days	
	Cape Horn to Equator	32	,,	
	Equator to Lizard	26	,,	
	Lizard to Cuxhaven	9	,,	
November 24	Arrived Cuxhaven	92	,,	out
		83	,,	to Lizard

THIRTEENTH VOYAGE.

March 9, 1910	Left Cuxhaven			
	Cuxhaven to Lizard	3	days	
	Lizard to Equator	19	,,	
	Equator to Cape Horn	32	,,	
	Cape Horn to Taltal	17	,,	
May 19	Arrived Taltal	68	,,	from Lizard
		71	,,	from Cuxhaven
June 3, 1910	Left Taltal			
	Taltal to Cape Horn	19	days	
	Cape Horn to Equator	28	,,	
	Equator to Lizard	28	,,	
	Lizard to Cuxhaven	2	,,	
August 19	Arrived Cuxhaven	77	,,	out

The Wreck of the "Preussen."

No firm of shipowners has been so unlucky in the matter of Channel collisions as Laeisz's "P" Line of nitrate clippers. In this way their finest ship was lost. On her fourteenth voyage the *Preussen* was proceeding down Channel under all sail when the Newhaven-Dieppe steamer, *Brighton*, gravely miscalculated her speed and tried to cross her bow instead of going under her stern.

The accident happened a little before midnight on Saturday, November 6, 1910. The night was hazy, and steamers were blowing their whistles, but the wind was freshening with a falling glass and the fog was thinning away.

Suddenly the Channel steamer was observed, and the mate of the *Preussen* only had time to cry out a warning before his ship ran into her. The *Brighton*, which was bound to Dieppe with 90 passengers, was struck on her port side abreast of the engine-room, but owing to the *Preussen* having a clipper bow she was only damaged above water, her port side being crushed in, the port lifeboat stove, the officers' cabins bashed in, and the mainmast snapped off at the deck. The *Preussen's* bowsprit was carried away, and she was holed forward.

For a short while the *Brighton* stood by the sailing ship, then on ascertaining that the latter was not likely to sink she put back to Newhaven, arriving there at 3 a.m. on Sunday morning. The Railway Company's tug was immediately sent out to find the *Preussen*, which in the meantime had run back to Dungeness Roads with her forward watertight compartment full of water and her hands at the pumps.

It was now blowing fresh from the south-east with every prospect of the quick arrival of a depression from the Atlantic. The *Preussen*, with all her head-gear gone, her bowsprit banging against the side, and her foremast swaying about with all the head-stays carried away, had too much way on when her anchors were let go off Dungeness, with the result that both cables parted and Captain Nissen was obliged to stand off to sea.

All Sunday morning the gale steadily increased, with driving rain. A couple of tugs managed to pass their ropes aboard the *Preussen* and made a desperate effort to make Dover harbour by the eastern entrance, but the wind was blowing dead on-shore and the weight of the heavy ship was too much for the tugs. In spite of their efforts she drifted closer and closer towards the cliffs, and finally struck at 4.30 p.m.

It was growing dark, the rain was coming down in torrents, the wind was blowing a hard gale at south-south-west, and the *Preussen*, lying broadside on to wind and sea, bumped heavily on the rocks throughout the night. At the first crash everything above her topsail yards at the fore came tumbling down, whilst the surf made a clean breach over the vessel.

A miserable night was passed by all aboard. The crew, wet to the skin and almost frozen, when not pumping, apparently spent their time under the foc's'le-head listening to the crash of the seas and wondering if their ship would hold together. Captain Nissen had cold meat and a tot of cognac served out to all hands. Little could be done except pump. The tide was rising, and with the wind blowing dead on shore the *Preussen* was soon little better than a half-tide rock. Although four tugs were in attendance it was blowing too hard for them to establish communication with the wreck, but ashore, as soon as it was known that the big ship was bumping close in under the high cliffs on the rocks of Crab Bay, frenzied attempts were made at a rescue.

The maroons were fired a little before 5 o'clock in order to summon the lifeboatmen and the rocket apparatus crews to their stations. When the *Preussen* was first noticed in the afternoon driving inshore it was thought that the tugs would be able to get their hawsers aboard in time and have power enough to haul her off, and thus the launch of the lifeboat was delayed and the rocket was not fired until 4.50 p.m.

The lifeboat, *Mary Hamar Hoyle,* stationed on the Marine Parade, was quickly manned by Coxswain Brockman and his crew. The crowd of anxious spectators manned the hauling off rope. The lifeboat stuck at first, but after a little delay got safely afloat. She was picked up by one of the Dover harbour tugs, the *Lady Vita,* and towed off to the *Preussen.* There was a big sea running, and this broke clean over the lifeboat, almost washing her crew from their seats, and it was soon realised that it would be dangerous for the tossing lifeboat to go alongside the *Preussen.* However, the tug took her up to windward of the wreck, and then, by easing away on the tow-line, dropped her down as near as was safe to the ship's quarter, where every sea washed over the lifeboat. Her crew shouted themselves hoarse, but could get no response from the *Preussen,* although they noticed that lights were burning in the deckhouses.

After this failure to establish communication, the *Mary Hamar Hoyle* was towed back to Dover harbour in the teeth of the gale, her crew landing a little before 9.30 p.m. after having had a most strenuous, not to say dangerous, experience.

Meanwhile two bodies of Coastguards with rocket apparatus, one lot from Dover and the other from St. Margaret's, made their way along the shore and the cliffs, the one party below and the other above. The cliffs here are about 200 feet high, and Coastguard Hughes volunteered to go down the face of the cliff by means of a rope ladder. This was no pleasant job in the gale that was blowing, and he was about half-way down when the lower party at the foot of the cliffs fired their rocket.

"DUNKERQUE"

Lent by the Nautical Photo Agency

[*See page* 118

"PAMIR" LEAVING SAN ANTONIO FOR ANTOFAGASTA

Lent by C. A. Finsterbusch

[*See page* 100

"MARTHE"

[*See page* 133

The shot was a good one, and it fell over the *Preussen's* main rigging, thus establishing communication between ship and shore.

From the cliffs the noise of the *Preussen* grinding on the rocks as she was lifted and thumped down by every breaker could be plainly heard. The wreck was also lit up in most ghostly fashion by the sweeping flash of the South Foreland lighthouse.

About 11 p.m. the *Preussen* began firing rockets of distress, whereupon the lifeboat was again manned and towed off to the scene of the wreck. For some time the coxswain manoeuvred vainly in the ticklish job of getting in touch with the *Preussen.* At last the lifeboat was dropped down near enough for shouted communications to be heard. Captain Nissen asked the coxswain to assist in taking hawsers from the wreck to the four tugs which were standing by, namely, the *Lady Vita, Lady Curzon, John Bull* and *Albatross.* This task was successfully carried out by the lifeboat, and the coxswain then offered to attempt the difficult business of taking off the *Preussen's* crew. This offer was not accepted, Captain Nissen and his officers evidently hoping that at high water the tugs would be able to float their stranded vessel; but from the very first those ashore, with their local knowledge, knew that she was doomed.

By daylight the following morning there were no less than twelve tugs in attendance on the stranded sailing ship, but with the gale still blowing and a big sea running there was nothing that they could do except stand by. As high water approached, the crew of the *Preussen* were obliged to take refuge on the bridge deck amidships, and even here they would have been swept overboard by the breaking surf if it had not been for the high rail.

During the whole of Monday little could be done. From 9 o'clock the lifeboat stood by along with the twelve tugs and salvage vessels—English, Belgian, Dutch and German. It was arranged that a last attempt to get the vessel off should be made at high tide on Monday afternoon, but not one of the waiting fleet was able to get a hawser aboard the *Preussen* owing to the heavy sea running, although the skippers, with that uncanny seamanship possessed by tugboatmen, manoeuvred again and again to get their vessels into position, and took risks which even the critical situation of the *Preussen* hardly warranted, and by two o'clock they were obliged to abandon their efforts—which had been watched by thousands of spectators gathered along the cliffs—and returned to Dover harbour.

By Tuesday morning all hope of salving the vessel was abandoned. After three nights without sleep and with the seas breaking over them, the crew were landed on Tuesday afternoon. The first Germans ashore were her two passengers, the one a sea painter and the other Dr. Budzier, an instructor at the Navigation School at Rostock. They were taken off by a Deal galley, which put them aboard the tug *Albatross*. The doctor, a typical German of thirty, short, stout, spectacled, was interviewed by the ubiquitous reporter as he walked off the pier carrying two small bags of clothing, which he had saved from the wreck.

"I go to Hamburg to seek another boat," he said in broken English. "We have had a dreadful time. Some food—yes, and luckily a little wine, for the water was brackish, but no sleep since three days, and the sea all over us."

Soon after this the tugboat *Lady Vita* towed a lighter off to the wreck, which took off 18 of the crew, and the remainder, consisting of 30 men, were brought ashore before dark.

A typical telegram from the Kaiser was received by Captain Nissen before the *Preussen* was abandoned, and this he proudly read out to his crew. The telegram ran as follows:

> Deeply moved by the news of the disaster of the proud five-master *Preussen*. I desire to express to the owners my warmest sympathy. I should like a direct report regarding the result of the catastrophe, and especially about the fate of the brave crew, which causes me much anxiety.

The reading of this telegram was received with three cheers by the drenched and bedraggled company aboard the wreck.

As soon as it was decided to give up all idea of floating the *Preussen*, as it was considered that there was danger of her breaking in two should any strain be put upon her by the tugs, lighters were got together in order to unload the cargo, which consisted of furnace coke, cement, wall-paper, wood, wax, earthenware, glassware, enamel ware, barbed wire, brown paper, string, school slates, lamps, ornaments and a number of German pianos. Most of this cargo, including a hundred pianos, was got safely ashore. Three salvage vessels were kept working upon the wreck until a fierce gale once more thumped her upon the rocks. This time the great ship's back was broken.

The systematic salvage of her masts, spars, sails, gear, etc., was continued until the war interrupted operations. By this time even her deckhouses and pitch-pine decks had been stripped from the hull. During the war half of the wreck broke off and disappeared. The remaining half, however, with one lower-mast standing, survived the war.

"Pangani" and "Petschili."

Apparently Herr Laeisz was content with his experiments in five-masted sailing ships, for he did not follow the *Potosi* and *Preussen* up with any further giants for the "P" fleet. Instead, he contented himself with the 3000-tonned four-mast barque, two of which type were launched for him in 1903, the *Pangani* by Tecklenborg, and the *Petschili* by Blohm & Voss.

The first captain of the *Pangani* was Captain T. Schmidt and he was followed by Captain F. Junge in 1907. On her maiden voyage this vessel arrived out at Valparaiso on June 15, 65 days out from Dungeness. Her return passage was made in 75 days from Iquique to the Isle of Wight. Her best outward passage was made in 1904, being 64 days from the Channel to Valparaiso, and her best homeward was from Mejillones to Scilly, 62 days in 1910.

The *Pangani* was the third of Laeisz's ships to be run into by a steamer, and the collision in this case ended in the sinking of the "P" clipper and the loss of all her crew except four men. The *Pangani* was run into by the steamer *Phryne* off Cape La Hogue when outward bound, and sank so rapidly that there was no time to launch a boat.

The best known commanders of the *Petschili* were Captain C. N. Preutzmann (who took her from the stocks), and Captain A. Teschner. Her best outward passage was made in 1905, 62 days from Dover to Talcahuano. Her best homeward run was 77 days from Taltal to Scilly in 1912.

"Pamir."

This beautiful 3000-ton four-mast barque, which was launched by Blohm & Voss in October, 1905, has proved herself to be quite the equal of any of her predecessors in making good regular passages. Her best voyage previous to the war was made in 1906 under Captain C. N. Preutzmann.

Scilly to Valparaiso	64 days
Iquique to Scilly	75 „

After the war she was allocated to the Italian Government, but was soon back in the "P" fleet, and distinguished herself in 1925 by making the smartest outward passage round the Horn accomplished since the war. She arrived at Talcahuano on May 14, 1925, 75 days from Hamburg and only 71 from the Ushant.

The start of her next outward passage was a most unpleasant one. Leaving Hamburg on December 20, 1925, she experienced frightful weather in the Channel and was forced at last to put into Falmouth. She was spoken near Dover on December 27, and on January 7, 1926, arrived in Carrick Roads, having lost three men overboard, both her anchors and the starboard chain, besides having had several sails blown to smithereens.

That year she raced home against the auxiliary *Magdalene Vinnen.*

The latter left Antofagasta on June 9, 1926, and *Pamir* left Iquique on the same day.

On August 4, *Pamir* was 2 degrees astern in Lat. 9° N., Long. 28° W., the auxiliary being in 11° N., 28° W. *Magdalene Vinnen* arrived at Granville on August 27, 79 days out, whilst *Pamir* passed Prawle Point on September 2, 86 days out, and reached Terneuzen on September 7. It is probable that the Diesel engine of *Magdalene Vinnen* just decided the race in her favour.

Since that date *Pamir's* passages have been most consistent, her best times being:

Left Talcahuano April 12, 1928 Arrived Ipswich July 4 83 days
Left Iquique November 13, 1928 Passed Prawle Pt. Feb. 7, 1929 86 „
She arrived Rotterdam in tow on February 16, being unable to reach Hamburg owing to the ice.

In 1929 *Pamir* left Hamburg on April 23, passed Ushant on April 30 and Madeira on May 10, and finally anchored at Talcahuano on July 7, having made the smart passage of 75 days from Hamburg and 68 from Ushant. She came home from Iquique in 87 days. Leaving that port on August 29, she passed the Falklands on September 23 and reached Bruges on November 24.

Bought Ships of the "P" Fleet.

Between 1907 and the outbreak of war Herr Laeisz purchased the following vessels:

British ship *Argo* ex *Brynymor*, 2118 tons, built by MacMillan, 1902, renamed *Peiho.*
Italian four-mast barque, *Regina Elina*, 2344 tons, built at Genoa, 1903, renamed *Ponape.*
British ship, *Fitzjames*, 1946 tons, built by Hamilton, 1902, renamed *Pinnas.*
German ship, *Osorno* ex *Beethoven*, 1789 tons, built Tecklenborg, 1894, renamed *Pirna.*
German four-mast barque, *Mneme*, 2423 tons, built by J. Reid, 1903, renamed *Pommern.*
German ship *Albert Rickmers*, 2039 tons, built by Rickmers, 1905, renamed *Penang.*
Italian four-mast barque, *Erasmo*, 2102 tons, built Riva Trigosa, 1903, renamed *Pinguin.*
British four-mast barque *Arrow*, 3084 tons, built by Rodger, 1902, renamed *Parma.*
British barque *Radiant*, 1971 tons, built by Rodger, 1903, renamed *Perim.*
German ship *Dione*, 2103 tons, built by Rijkee, Rotterdam, 1905, renamed *Pelikan.*

We may be quite sure that the shrewd German shipowner had a keen eye for a good ship and was not to be led into buying an indifferent vessel owing to an attractive price, thus these purchased "P" liners should be of special interest as being exceptionally fine specimens of latter day sailing ships.

Two of them were oil sailers and fetched a big price, the *Arrow* costing Laeisz £15,000 and the *Radiant* £10,000. They were both bought in 1911. The fine British full-rigger *Fitzjames* was bought in 1909 for £8000 or at the rate of £4 7s. 0d. per ton.

The Sister Ships "Peking" and "Passat."

This beautiful pair, which were launched by Blohm & Voss in May and November, 1911, were about 100 tons larger than *Pamir.*

Both vessels proved themselves capable of doing an 80-day passage either way. On November 30, 1912, the *Peking* under Captain Nissen left Hamburg for Valparaiso, but was obliged to put back to Cuxhaven with damage to her windlass received during very heavy weather in the North Sea. Leaving Cuxhaven again on December 5, she reached Valparaiso on February 24, 1913, 81 days out. *Passat,* under Captain Wendler, put up a still better outward passage before the war. She left Hamburg on September 29, 1912, and arrived Valparaiso December 11, 73 days out.

Both vessels have put up some very fine records since the war, which I have included in the passage table.

F. Laeisz loses his Fleet owing to the War.

The war cost Herr Laeisz his whole fleet. The *Ponape* was the first victim. She was captured in 1914 and taken into Falmouth. She later became one of the short-lived line of J. Bell & Co., being renamed *Bellhouse.*

The ***Pelikan*** was also bought by J. Bell & Co. and renamed *Bellco.*

Parma and *Peiho* were allocated to the British Government. Besides *Potosi,* the French received *Pinnas* and *Passat,* whilst the Italians took over *Perim, Pamir, Peking* and *Pirna* renamed *Pinus.*

Pommern went to the Greek Government, and *Penang* hoisted the flag of John Nurminen of Danzig.

The great German shipowner, however, was not to be crushed out of existence by the simple method of confiscating his fleet. He at once set about buying back the pick of his ships from their new owners, who had no idea what to do with them and were only too glad to receive marks instead of ships.

In this way *Peiho, Parma, Pamir, Passat, Pinnas* and *Peking* returned to their old flag, and by 1922 the famous "P" Line was once more in being.

"Priwall" and "Padua."

Not only was Herr Laeisz not satisfied with getting his old ships back, but he began building again.

It is evident that the famous Hamburg firm have satisfied themselves that the most economical form of sailing ship is the four-mast barque of about 3000 tons gross, and no more experiments have been made in five-mast ships and barques in spite of the example of the queerly rigged "Vinnens."

In 1918 Messrs. Blohm & Voss built the four-mast barque *Priwall* of 2849 tons net.

In June 24, 1926, Tecklenborg launched the splendid *Padua* at Wesermunde.

Designed to carry 4800 tons of deadweight on a net regis-

"VALENTINE"

Lent by J. Randall

[*See page* 123.

"ANTONIN"

Lent by Mons. Antonin Bordes

[*See page* 136

tered tonnage of 2678, the *Padua* may be considered the very latest development of the trader depending upon sails alone. Her sail area, it was stated, totalled 36,500 square feet; plenty of canvas for a four-mast barque of that size, but like everything else in her design, by no means out of the way.

Wise in their generation the Germans insist that their officers shall be sail trained, and accommodation was provided on the *Padua* for 40 cadets.

Only recently I had a sad letter from Chile lamenting the decay of the British sailor and remarking that amongst foreigners the British officer was now considered inferior on all points to the sail-trained Germans, Finns, Danes and Souwegians generally. And this inferiority was put down to their ignorance of the primordial ways of the sea; in other words, they were navigators and engineers but not seamen or men of the sea.

"Padua's" Maiden Voyage.

Padua sailed from Hamburg on August 30, 1926, under Captain Petersen, the most experienced perhaps of all Laeisz's captains and best remembered as the Commander of the famous *Preussen*. Finisterre was passed on September 15, 16 days out. After being spoken in 28° 42′ N., 18° 32′ W., on September 24; on October 17 in 8° 44′ S., 29° W., and on November 19 in 45° S., 78° W., the "P" liner reached Talcahuano 87 days out from Hamburg, 71 days from Finisterre. She sailed from Taltal loaded with nitrate on January 5, 1927; was spoken off the Horn 29 days out; was in 5° S., 30° W., on March 7, 61 days out; and arrived at Delfzijl on April 9, 94 days out.

Her second and third voyages showed still better work.

"Padua's" Second Voyage.

Padua sailed from Hamburg on June 15, 1927; was obliged to anchor in Sandown Bay on June 26 for medical assistance; on June 30 passed Finisterre 17 days out; was in the latitude of Madeira on July 3, was spoken July 19 in 6° N., 18° W., 34 days out (20 days from Finisterre); and again on July 30, in 19° 10′ S., 36° 20′ W.; on August 14 she was in 44° S., 59° W.; and arrived at Talcahuano on September 5, 82 days out and 68 days from Finisterre.

This voyage he loaded at Iquique, and sailing on October 27, 1927, was in 52° S., 55° W. on November 15, 29 days out; on December 10 she was in 3° 46′ S., 29° 33′ W., 54 days out; passed Dover on January 10, 1928, 85 days out; and arrived at Hamburg on the 12th 87 days out.

"Padua's" Third Voyage.

This was truly a splendid performance; in these degenerate days of seamanship, there is, indeed, nothing degenerate in the sailing of the Laeisz ships; they are fit to be compared with any of their predecessors whose names and performances have been published throughout the world.

Padua sailed from Hamburg on April 5, 1928; passed Scilly on April 10; and was spoken in 16° N., 26° W., 24 days out on April 29; on May 20 she was in 24° S., 40° W., 45 days out; and on June 1, 55 days out in 45° S., 63° W. Talcahuano was reached on June 20, 76 days out, 71 days from Scilly and 45 days from the Equator.

This voyage she sailed from Mejillones on August 1, 1928; on August 21 she was in 53° S., 55° W., 20 days out, and only 24 hours astern of the *Priwall* which was 25 days out from

Iquique on August 20; on September 8 she was in 4° S., 28° W., 38 days out; was off Cape Clear on October 9, 69 days out; and arrived Terneuzen on October 12, 72 days out. This is undoubtedly the fastest voyage made by a sailing ship since the war.

"Passat's" Collisions.

It is an extraordinary fact that the beautiful run and superbly navigated "P" liners, which have shown themselves able to withstand the worst gales of the Horn and North Atlantic, have always been singularly unlucky in the matter of collisions.

Steamer captains never seemed able to gauge the speed of Herr Laeisz's tall ships as they race up and down the Channel and the North Sea.

The latest victim of these collisions has been the *Passat.*

On August 15, 1928, the *Passat* left Hamburg; on the 25th when 20 miles S.W. of Dungeness and in clear weather, the French steamer *Daphne* tried to cross her bows, was cut down and sank in 10 minutes, her crew being saved and landed at Dungeness.

Passat with stem damaged and forepeak flooded was towed back to Rotterdam where she arrived on August 27. She was repaired and the voyage resumed on September 2.

On her next voyage *Passat* left Hamburg on June 20, 1929; and on June 25 was in collision with a steamer off the *Royal Sovereign.* Again she was towed back to Rotterdam, this time by the tug *Hermes.*

After a second repair she left Rotterdam on July 18; was off Finisterre on July 26; abreast of Teneriffe on July 31; off Fernando Noronha on August 18; in the latitude of Bahia

Blanca on September 6; was off the Magellan Straits on September 11; and arrived Talcahuano on October 1, 47 days from Rotterdam.

This fine passage was beaten in 1930, when she passed the Isle of Wight on April 19 and reached Talcahuano on July 1, 73 days from the Wight.

The End of "Pinnas."

The last of Herr Laeisz's full-riggers was the *Pinnas*, the old British *Fitzjames*. After buying her back from the French the great German shipowner refitted her like a yacht. In July, 1923, she arrived in Southampton, beautifully fitted throughout with all wire running gear and was greatly admired. She is, however, the only one of the "P" ships which has come to grief since the war. She left Hamburg on January 22, 1929, and was abandoned dismasted off the Chilean coast on April 27, her crew being saved by the Chilean Government steamer *Alfonso*.

This disaster left *Parma* the only British built ship in the fleet.

"Parma's" Record since 1924.

Parma ex *Arrow* sailed from Hamburg on November 18, 1924; was off the Lizard on November 20; abreast of Madeira on November 30; and spoken on December 22 in 5° S., 32° W., 33 days out; on February 2, 1925, she was in 49° S., 78° W., and reached San Antonio 95 days out on February 11. Loading nitrate at Iquique she sailed on May 2, 1925; was 29 days out in 54° S., 55° W. on May 31; crossed the Equator in 28° W. on June 23, 53 days out; called at Fayal on July 20, 79 days out;

passed Dover on July 30, 89 days out; and reached Hamburg on August 2, 92 days out.

She sailed again from Hamburg on September 15, passed Ventnor, Isle of Wight, on September 25, and Finisterre on September 30, 15 days out. On October 31 she was in 4° S., 32° W., 46 days out; and was spoken in 52° S., 61° W., on November 29, 75 days out; reaching Corral on December 22, 85 days out from Finisterre and 98 days out from Hamburg.

She sailed from Mejillones on February 13, 1926, was 34 days out in 52° S., 55° W.; on April 17, 63 days out, in 6° S., 32° W.; off the North Foreland on May 30, 106 days out; and arrived Hamburg on June 3, 110 days out.

Hamburg was left on July 11, 1926; she was off Niton on July 16; and in 16° N., 22° W., on August 1, 21 days out. She was spoken on August 18 in 5° S., 30° W., 38 days out; and in 38° S., 55° W., on September 9, 59 days out. She was 9 days rounding the Horn, being spoken in 51° S., 80° W., on September 26, 77 days out; and reached Talcahuano on October 5, 86 days out.

On the homeward passage *Parma* left Iquique on November 20; was in 52° 20′ S., 55° W., on December 22, 32 days out; on January 23, 1927, was in 4° S., 29° W., 64 days out; on February 11 was in 38° N., 31° W., 83 days out; passed Dover on February 21, 93 days out; and reached Hamburg on February 23, 95 days out.

On March 26 sailed from Hamburg; was off Wick on March 30; spoken on April 23 in 16° N., 26° W., 28 days out; and again on May 19 in 23° S., 40° W., 54 days out. She passed through Le Maire Straits on June 9, 75 days out; took 8 days rounding the Horn, being in 50° S., 79° W., on June 17, 83 days out; and arrived at Talcahuano on June 22, 88 days out.

On August 20, *Parma* sailed from Taltal; was in 51° S., 52° W., on September 13, 24 days out; in 6° S., 26° W., on October 1, 42 days out; in 14° N., 28° W., 56 days out, on October 15; and in 40° N., 32° W., 73 days out, on November 1; she arrived Delfzijl on November 27, 99 days out.

Hamburg was left again on January 1, 1928; on January 4 when off Lowestoft she came into collision with a trawler and lost an anchor; was off Land's End on January 21; in 17° N., 26° W., on February 7; and in 9° S., 33° W., on February 18, having made a 20 days run from Land's End to the Equator. On February 26 she was spoken in 25° S., 41° W., and again reported on March 12 in 53° S., 64° W., 71 days out; on March 28 she was in 45° S., 78° W., and reached Talcahuano on April 1, 91 days out, but only 70 days from Land's End.

She sailed from Iquique on June 9, 1928, and was in 52° S., 54° W., when 30 days out; on August 8 was reported in 4° N., 27° W., 60 days out; on September 3 was 86 days out, 720 miles S.W. of Land's End; passed Dover on September 10, 93 days out, and arrived at Delfzijl on September 14, 97 days out.

On October 19, 1928, *Parma* left Hamburg for Talcahuano; was off Niton on October 29, and passed Finisterre on November 2, 14 days out. She was abreast of Cape Verde 25 days out, and off Fernando Noronha on November 24, 36 days out. On December 13, *Parma* was in 44° S., 62° W., 55 days out, and arrived at Talcahuano on January 7, 1929, 80 days out, but only 66 days from Finisterre, a remarkable passage for such a full-built ship. She left Tocopilla on March 1, passed Dover on June 5, and reached Ostend on June 8, 86 days out.

On her next voyage *Parma* left Hamburg on August 17; was off Dover on 23rd and the Canaries on September 12.

She reached Talcahuano on November 25, 100 days out. Iquique was left on January 3, 1930, and Prawle Point passed on April 12, 99 days out.

Ant. Dom. Bordes.

There is only one firm that could be compared in any way with that of F. Laeisz in the nitrate trade and that is the famous French firm of Ant. Dom. Bordes et Fils, whose ships were quite worthy to be compared with the best of the "P" Line.

This firm was founded as far back as 1847 by Monsieur Antonin Dominique Bordes.

Unfortunately the books of the firm previous to 1868 have been destroyed, but until that date M. Bordes had a partner named Le Quellec. When Le Quellec died in 1868 Ant. Dom. Bordes became the sole proprietor of this magnificent fleet of sailing ships and at once launched out with a big building programme.

The early ships were wooden three-masters of from 500 to 1000 tons burthen. They carried mixed cargoes and passengers from Bordeaux to Valparaiso, but at that date were unable to get full homeward cargoes of nitrate.

Amongst the very early ships were the first *Antonin*, *l'Anita*, *Eugenie* and the *St. Vincent de Paul.*

A curious legend was spread through the world about the Bordes ships owing to the name of this vessel.

The Jesuit Legend.

At the opening of the Suez Canal in 1869 all the wise-acres prophesied the speedy extinction of sailing ships; yet to the wonder of shipping people in the French ports, A. D. Bordes at this very moment began to buy a number of small iron barques and ships from the Clyde and other British builders.

No one was willing to believe that A. D. Bordes was ready to risk his whole fortune in sailing ship tonnage at such a time, and it was spread far and wide that the Bordes fleet belonged in reality to the religious Order of the Jesuits, for whom Ant. Dom. Bordes simply acted as an agent.

This legend became so firmly established that the son of M. Bordes heard it repeated long afterwards in such diverse spots as the West Indies, Brazil and Peru.

Force was lent to this legend by the name of the Bordes' ship, *St. Vincent de Paul.* This, it will be noticed, happens to be the only ship in the whole of the Bordes fleet from first to last that was called after a Saint, with the single exception of the steel barque *Jeanne d'Arc.* And this vessel was not christened by A. D. Bordes, being over 10 years old when she came under the firm's house-flag.

It will be noticed also that just before the war the firm bought the two large four-mast barques *Sainte Catherine* and *Sainte Marguerite,* but quickly changed their names to *Seine* and *Blanche.*

A. D. Bordes buys British Ships.

On the death of his partner, A. D. Bordes seems to have at once begun to reform his fleet and bring it up to date. He was one of those far-sighted, self-reliant men who act according to their own judgment, indifferent alike to the warnings of the pessimist or the over-confident advice of the optimist.

"EUROPE." (TAKEN DURING THE WAR)

Lent by Nautical Photo Agency

[*See page* 138

"CAROLINE" EX "MUSKOKA"

Lent by Capt. L. R. W. Beavis

[*See page* 137

Though he clung to sail bottoms at a time when many a shipowner was launching out into steam auxiliaries with disastrous consequences, A. D. Bordes was not wedded to the wooden hull, like some of his British contemporaries such as Dicky Green of the Blackwall Line, and his order to British firms was for iron vessels. These were all small handy iron ships and barques, not one of which exceeded 800 tons. At that date, 1868/9, it was rare to see a ship of over 1000 tons on the West Coast; such a large vessel indeed found a difficulty in filling her holds with homeward cargo unless she was ready to load guano.

Between 1868 and 1870 the following ships were built for A. D. Bordes in British yards:

Blanche and Louise	iron barque	581	tons	built by	Bowdler, Liverpool
Caroline ..	,, ,,	680		,,	Stephen, Glasgow
Adolphe ..	,, ,,	675		,,	Aitken, Glasgow
Alexandre ..	,, ,,	683		,,	Aitken, Glasgow
Valentin ..	,, ship	723		,,	Pearse, Stockton
Irene	,, ,,	722		,,	Pearse, Stockton
Bio-Bio ..	,, ,,	682		,,	Aitken, Glasgow
Gers	,, ,,	723		,,	Pearse, Stockton
Antonin ..	,, ,,	700		,,	Dobie, Glasgow
Seine	,, ,,	735		,,	Pearse, Stockton
Aconcagua ..	,, ,,	691		,,	Laird, Birkenhead
Tarapaca ..	,, ,,	692		,,	Dobie, Glasgow
Almendral ..	,, ,,	712		,,	Laird, Birkenhead

I give them in order of date.

Blanche and Louise was launched in December, 1868, and *Almendral* in June, 1870. These little vessels were designed to carry 1200 tons of 1000 kilos. Early iron ships were built of very thick plates and lasted, according to Lloyd's, much longer than the later steel ships.

Most of the above list were still afloat at the beginning of the 20th century. *Blanche and Louise* was sold by the firm in 1898, *Caroline* was destroyed by fire in 1893, *Adolphe* was lost in 1880, *Alexandre* was sold in 1901, *Valentin* went missing in 1885, *Irene* was lost in 1890, *Bio-Bio* disappeared in 1888, and *Antonin* in 1892. *Gers* was sold in 1898, *Aconcagua* went missing in 1890, *Seine* was sold in 1895 and *Almendral* in 1899, *Tarapaca* was lost in 1882.

I should have added two more names to their list.

Garonne		692 tons built Glasgow in 1870
Maipu	..	681 tons built Glasgow in 1870

These two were very short-lived, *Garonne* going missing in 1871 and *Maipu* in 1872.

Bordes' Early French-built Wooden Ships.

Of his wooden French-built ships A. D. Bordes retained seven small vessels and two of over 1000 tons. These were:

Valparaiso ..	470 tons	built	Bordeaux	1849	sold 1876
Maputeo ..	364	„	Sainte Terre	1853	lost 1881
Perseverance ..	709	„	Bordeaux	1855	lost 1877
Chili	1277	„	„	1856	sold 1883
Victorine ..	1621	„	„	1858	lost 1875
Casimir Le Quellac	502	„	„	1863	sold 1886
Cap Horn ..	553	„	„	1865	lost 1877
Blanche ..	599	„	„	1867	sold 1887
Francois Joseph	506	„	La Roque	1867	sold 1887

Cargoes in the Early Days.

Bordes' ships in the sixties and seventies loaded general cargo and passengers at Bordeaux, for Valparaiso—and it often took some months before a return cargo could be loaded. The export of nitrate was in its infancy, and there was often insufficient to make a complete cargo; also lighters were scarce and the methods of the stevedores excessively slow. Most of Bordes' early homeward cargoes were landed in British ports; this, of course, did not please an enterprising man of A. D. Bordes' calibre, and in 1870 he imported the first cargo of nitrate into France for the benefit of French agriculture. But the old man did not live to see the full fruits of his foresight. In 1882 he took his three sons into the business and the style of the firm became Ant. Dom. Bordes et Fils.

Just a year later, on May 28, 1883, to be exact, old A. D. Bordes died.

But his policy with all its enterprise and business acumen was carried on with ever greater success by the sons. Before long they established depots for nitrate at Dunkerque, Nantes, La Rochelle, Bordeaux and also in the interior of France.

And each year the tonnage of the fleet and the size of the ships increased. During the later seventies a number of small wooden barques were added to the fleet, the tonnage being still kept small by the scarcity of nitrate.

Additions to the Fleet in the Seventies.

These little ships were all built in French yards, their names being:

Bordeaux	..	639 tons	built	La Roque	1872	sold 1884
Valentine	..	642	,,	La Roque	1872	sold 1884
Montmorency	..	610	,,	La Roque	1872	sold 1884
Coquimbo	..	726	,,	La Roque	1873	sold 1884
Cerro Alegre	..	608	,,	La Roque	1873	sold 1889
Garonne	..	863	,,	Bordeaux	1873	missing 1882
Agustin Edwards		1010	,,	Bordeaux	1873	sold 1889
Quillota	..	723	,,	La Roque	1874	sold 1888
Chanaral	..	729	,,	La Roque	1874	sold 1888
Rancagua Bravo		712	,,	La Roque	1874	sold 1886

Bernadino ..	1022 tons	built	Bordeaux	1874	sold 1890
Marseille ..	687	,,	La Roque	1875	sold 1888
Havre	639	,,	Bordeaux	1875	sold 1888
Pacifique ..	851	,,	Bordeaux	1875	lost 1885
Maipu ..	679	,,	La Roque	1876	sold 1887
Centre Amerique	633	,,	La Roque	1876	sold 1890
San Francisco ..	656	,,	La Roque	1876	sold 1890
Buenos Ayres ..	649	,,	La Roque	1876	sold 1887

As the names in the Bordes fleet were continued from ship to ship, it is important to note the date of sale or loss, otherwise it is difficult not to get confused.

There is one other point to note about the names of A. D. Bordes' ships, they show very clearly the wide ramifications of the firm's business with the South American Continent.

Besides the wooden ships, by 1880 nine more iron ships had been added to the fleet. These were:

Emilie ex *Robert Mackenzie*	858 tons	built	Glasgow	1860	sold 1890
Carioca	775	,,	Nantes	1866	,, 1903
Tijuca	684	,,	,,	1867	,, 1907
Apolline Emilie	710	,,	Le Seyne	1868	,, 1894
Breiz Tzel	388	,,	Nantes	1869	,, 1888
Tamaris	476	,,	La Seine	1868	lost 1887
Glaneuse	482	,,	,,	1870	,, 1886
Valparaiso (2)	1239	,,	Glasgow (by Macfayden)	1874	sold 1900
Victorine (2) ..	1217	,,	Dundee (by Stephen)	1879	sunk by a German submarine in 1917.

All these small iron ships could sail; indeed, the little *Carioca* just before she was sold put up two sailing records which were equal to the best of those made by vessels three times her size. On November 7, 1898, she arrived at St. Pierre only 63 days out from Tocopilla, and in 1902 she arrived out in Coquimbo on July 15, just 68 days out from Cardiff.

Tijuca in the following year made a great effort to beat *Carioca's* passage from Wales to Coquimbo, but she failed by 8 days, arriving on June 23, 76 days out from Barry. This ship's best homeward passage was made in 1901, Iquique to St. Pierre, arriving December 20, 78 days out. It is interesting to note that *Carioca* arrived at St. Pierre on January 13, 87 days out from Iquique, so that *Tijuca* made the better passage of the two.

Apolline Emilie's best passage out to the West Coast was made in 73 days. She left Bordeaux on November 28, 1893, and arrived Valparaiso on February 9, 1894.

Victorine's best outward passage, made from Dartmouth to Valparaiso in the spring of 1893, was just a day better.

Valparaiso's best passage was a homeward one, from Pisagua to the Lizard in 81 days, when she made her number on May 28, 1894. This vessel will be remembered by old British seamen as the *Workington.* She had already changed hands more than once when A. D. Bordes bought her, her other names being *Port of Monte Video* and *Sufren.*

Bordes' First Four-masters.

In September, 1882, Russell & Co. launched the 2139-tonned iron four-master *Union* at Greenock. She was built to the order of A. D. Bordes and was his first ship of over 2000 tons. But the nitrate trade was now increasing by leaps and bounds, and the *Union* was quickly followed by three more iron four-masters. These were all built in Thomson's yard at Glasgow:—*A. D. Bordes* of 2230 tons in 1884, *Perseverance* of 2511 tons, and *Tarapaca* of 2408 tons in 1886. None of these four vessels put up such good sailing records as Bordes' later French-built ships, the *A. D. Bordes* with a passage of 70 days from Dover to Valparaiso in 1899 being perhaps the best performer.

The big *Perseverance* did not last very long, being posted missing in 1892.

The *Union* was A. D. Bordes' first loss in the war, being sunk by a German cruiser in 1914.

The *Tarapaca* followed her to the bottom in 1917, being the victim of a German submarine.

Bordes' War Losses.

It is doubtful if any firm suffered greater losses from enemy action in actual ships than that of A. D. Bordes.

Between 1914 and 1919 this magnificent fleet of sailing ships was diminished by 22 vessels and over 50,000 tons.

The only steamer under Bordes' house-flag, the *Magellan*, of 6265 tons net, was also sunk by a German submarine.

Bordes' First Steel Ships.

These were also British-built four-mast barques.

In 1888 the *Cap Horn*, 2608 tons, came from Russell's yard. She was followed in the same year by the *Dunkerque* of 2987 tons and from the same builders. Then in 1889 came the *Nord*, of 2905 tons, from one of Barclay Curle's slips.

The *Dunkerque* went missing in 1891, but both *Cap Horn* and *Nord* were still afloat when the firm began to sell their sailing ships in 1923.

The best passage that I can find of these three British-built ships is one of 71 days from Iquique to St. Catherine's, Isle of Wight, made by the *Nord* in 1892.

Cap Horn's best seems to have been 73 days from Iquique to Dunkirk 10 years later.

The Five-master "France."

It was A. D. Bordes and not F. Laeisz as is often supposed who had the enterprise and daring to build the first five-masted square-rigged sailing ship, for on September 2, 1890, the *France* was launched from D. & W. Henderson's yard at Partick, having been constructed to Bordes' special requirements for carrying nitrate.

Her measurements were as follows:—Length registered 361 feet; breadth registered 48 feet 8 inches; depth registered 25 feet 9 inches; moulded depth 30 feet. Her tonnage was gross 3800, net 3326, and her deadweight capacity was considered to be 6200 tons, though I do not believe she ever loaded this weight, being well down to her marks on her maiden passage with 5900 tons of coal on board.

Her freeboard appeared low when compared to her length, but her fine sheer gave her a look of power and she certainly was a very handsome vessel. Her sheer was by no means so pronounced as that of the second French five-master *France*, whose foredeck was so steep that you could toboggan down it in wet weather.

The first *France's* sail area was 49,000 square feet; this with masts 160 feet from deck to truck, lower yards of 85 feet and royal yards of 48 feet was by no means excessive as sail plans went in those days, when Glasgow shipbuilders were being tempted to allow a dangerously low margin of safety in their stability tables owing to their desire for big sail areas. With iron yards, big chains and wires aloft, the weight and leverage on the box-like hulls of these big steel four-posters was tremendous, and many of the *France's* contemporaries actually did capsize, whilst others disappeared or were dismasted on their maiden voyages.

Though far less extreme aloft than most, the *France* certainly was considered rather crank and always required careful handling. Yet she had a cellular double bottom, holding 2000 tons of water ballast. Into this tank the drainings from the nitrate cargo were allowed to run, these being therefore saved to the owners, instead of being pumped overboard according to the usual custom in the nitrate trade.

The big ship had only two steel decks and her immense hold only had the usual collision bulkhead forward.

In order to be able to load and discharge with despatch, the *France* was given four steam winches for each hatch. Her record for quick work in this respect was the discharging of 5000 tons of coal and loading 5500 tons of nitrate at Iquique in eleven days.

Her windlass was also worked by steam, and where possible her running gear was of wire, also her standing rigging was set up by screws instead of the old time deadeyes and lanyards.

Her crew all told numbered 46 hands. On her maiden passage she showed that she possessed a good turn of speed by going from Barry to Rio in 32 days.

Then in 1892 she left Shields on March 26 and arrived out in Valparaiso Bay on June 10, only 71 days from Beachy Head and 76 from Shields. This fine passage she repeated on her next voyage. Leaving Newcastle on December 4, she was off Prawle Point on the 7th and reached Valparaiso on February 18, 1893, 73 days from Prawle Point.

"GENERAL NEUMAYER"

[*See page* 138

"GENERAL NEUMAYER"

[*See page* 138

"VALPARAISO"

[*See page* 136

"JEANNE D'ARC"

Lent by Captain L. R. W. Beavis

[*See page* 139

Then in 1895 we find her leaving Dunkirk on December 23, and reaching Iquique on March 8, 1896, only 75 days out. In the autumn of that year with 6000 tons of nitrate, she made the Channel from Iquique on the 79th day out. On the night of Monday, January 25, 1897, she brought up in Dungeness Roads, on her way to Dunkirk, her discharging port. It was a clear night, but unfortunately besides her riding light she had a lantern hung over her stern.

It happened that H.M.S. *Blenheim* was steaming up Channel at 13 knots, and she mistook the two lights of the *France* for those of fishing boats, so she set a course to steer between them. The wild shouts of the Frenchmen and the looming up of the giant hull were almost too late to save the *France.* At the last moment the *Blenheim's* helm was put hard over, luckily she was a handy ship and quick on her helm, and the *France* only received a glancing blow on her starboard quarter. Nevertheless the sharp cutwater of the man-of-war went clean through the *France's* plates into the captain's cabin, and considerable damage was done to her rails, bulwarks and upper plates.

Such a curious case aroused a great deal of attention, and in shipping circles there was much argument as to who was to blame.

Of course the case went to Court, where Lord Esher ruled that "the riding light forward was necessary and sufficient, and the stern light a source of error, which might cause or contribute to an accident." The Admiralty were glad to avoid a court-martial by adopting a similar view. What Mons. A. D. Bordes thought of British justice and seamanship would, I expect, make unpleasant reading for a nation which rather prides itself on both qualities.

However the *France* was repaired and on her very next outward passage made the best time of her career, being only 63 days from Prawle Point to Valparaiso.

She made two more passages in the seventies. On October 28, 1900, she arrived at Iquique 76 days from Prawle Point; and in 1901 she came home from Iquique in 78 days.

She sailed outwards again on March 14, 1901, with 5108 tons of Tyne coal for Valparaiso. And the next news of her came two months later when the barque *Josepha* reported passing the great five-master deserted, on her beam ends and with the sea sweeping over her decks.

A pampero had apparently proved to be too much for her. And so the first five-master came to her end.

Bordes buys old British Ships.

The loss of their great ship must have been a severe blow to the great French firm, which since her launch had contented itself with picking up bargains in the British sale market instead of ordering new ships, as the list on page 123 will show.

M. Bordes also bought one German ship, the *Libussa*, an iron ship of 1526 tons, which he renamed *Strasbourg*. This fine vessel came to her end by dismasting in 1914.

It will be noticed that except for the *Marthe* ex *Melita*, which only lasted a very short time under Bordes' house-flag, and the well known *Knight of St. Michael*, renamed *Pacifique*, none of these bought ships was of any size, and it was undoubtedly the French sailing ship bounty which gave the famous firm a mighty shove forward whilst it slowly put her foreign rivals out of business.

BRITISH SHIPS BOUGHT BY A. D. BORDES.

British Name	French Name	Tons net.	End of
River Clyde ..	*Valentine* (3)	741	Sold 1892
Mallowdale ..	*Adolphe*	1169	Sold 1901
Berkshire	*Pacifique* (2)	1281	Lost 1895
Cochrina	*Coquimbo*	911	Sold 1903
Ariadne	*Valentine* (4)	1167	Lost 1898
Tilkhurst	*Blanche* (2)	1527	Sold 1903
Killean	*Antonin* (3)	1660	Sold 1901
Nereus	*Aconcagua* (2)	1194	Sunk by German submarine, 1917
Martin Scott ..	*Chanaral*	1388	Capsized and foundered January 1902.
Brahmin	*Quillota* (2)	1264	Lost 1901
Melita	*Marthe*	2658	Lost 1898
Slieve Bawn ..	*Rancagua*	1443	Sold 1901
Skelmorlie	*Cerro Alegre* (2)	1436	Sold 1914
Knight of St. Michael	*Pacifique* (3)	2055	Sold 1916

French Sailing Ship Bounties.

The French Navigation Bounties, as they were called, which came into being just before the end of the nineteenth century, amounted to 1 franc 70 cents per gross ton per 1000 miles.

In addition to this, building bounties helped the lucky French sailing ship owners to add to their fleets. The sailing bounty was paid on the gross tonnage. French shipping people could afford to go in for nicely lined vessels, and make up their bounty rates by as much superstructure as possible, thus we find many of the latter day French sailing ships with practically an extra deck, their poops extending forward to within a few feet of the topgallant foc's'le bulkhead. And the difference between their gross and net tonnage was tremendous. Let me give a few examples.

A. D. Bordes' *Dunkerque*, which was built by La Porte at Rouen and launched in February, 1897, had a gross tonnage of 3338 tons and net of 2498, a difference of 840 tons. Her poop deck was 85 feet long and her foc's'le-head 61 feet besides a break of 11 feet.

The steel ship *Amiral Cecille*, built in 1902 by the Chantiers et Ateliers de St. Nazaire, Rouen, for the Societe Nouvelle d'Armement of Nantes, registered 2847 tons gross and only 1874 net. She had a poop 136 feet long, midship bridge of 44 feet and foc's'le-head of 49 feet, totalling 229 feet out of a length of 282 feet 8 inches.

Then there was the famous steel three-mast barque, *Marguerite Molinos*, built at Havre in 1897 and owned by the Societe des Voilers Francais. She registered 2005 tons gross and only 1567 net, with a poop 56 feet long and foc's'le-head of 39.

The Case of the "Marguerite Molinos."

This beautiful vessel deserves more than a passing word, for she was undoubtedly one of the smartest sailing ships under the tricolour. As her builders received 130,325 francs as a building bounty, she only cost her owners 515,082 francs

In her first year of work, between October 1897, and November 1898, she made three passages under Captain Mahe, and her profit amounted to nearly half her cost—to be exact, to 47 per cent. of it.

She first of all took 2500 tons of coal from Cardiff to San Francisco at a freight of 51,875 francs. From San Francisco she came back to Havre with 2450 tons of wheat, for which she received 91,875 francs, and, incidentally, she made the passage from San Francisco to Falmouth in 90 days.

Her next passage was with coal to Majunga for 29,605 francs, expenses deducted.

After deducting 5333 francs for management charges; 10,095 francs for interest on borrowed capital; 3350 francs as present to her master; 29,375 francs for expenses on first voyage, her net earnings for the three passages came to 125,202 francs. To this the navigation bounty must be added. The mileage of the three passages was 13,551, 13,627 and 7743 miles respectively. Thus the bounty of 1 franc 70 cents per 1000 miles added up to 119,028 francs. This when added to the net freight of 125,202 francs shows a profit of 244,230 francs for the 12 months.

A. D. Bordes' *Jacqueline*, on her maiden voyage, did almost equally well. She left Marseilles ballasted with tiles for Australia—they considered tiles no better than ballast in those good old days; from Australia she crossed to the West Coast and loaded nitrate home; her bounty for nine months' sailing totalling 160,000 francs. Under such conditions French sailing ship owners could afford to be indifferent about such small matters as bad freights.

But we need not be surprised to find British sailing ship owners in a mood of desperation banding themselves together into a Union in the vain hope of being able to fix minimum rates of freight for sail cargoes.

Undoubtedly these French bounties were the main factor in causing a panic-like rush to sell their ships on the part of British shipowners, which gradually increased in intensity as more and more new bounty-fed Frenchmen were sent afloat.

But there was some jealousy even amongst the lucky French shipowners, and Messrs. A. D. Bordes were accused of taking an undue share of the bounty. It was declared that out of 10,500,000 francs allotted as sailing ship bounties during the first 59 months the bounty had become law, that is up to the end of 1897, that the great firm had received nearly two-fifths of it.

In reply to this, Bordes et Fils averred that it required 6,500,000 to maintain and run their enormous fleet and that the bounty received by them came to barely one-sixth of this amount.

Bordes' Bounty Ships.

The French nation have always been celebrated for their skill in the designing and building of ships. And this has been the case right back to the days of Louis XIV. French ships, whether men-of-war or merchantmen, have always been noted for their good looks and their good sailing powers. And when the bounty-fed boom swept through the shipyards of France in the nineties of the last century, though construction may sometimes have been on the light side, good looks, speed and seaworthiness still clung as of yore to French designs.

As regards looks, few vessels could compete with A. D. Bordes' nitrate clippers with their white masts and spars and line of painted ports running just below the covering board. A member of Bordes' fleet could be spotted at sea at almost any distance owing to her smart appearance. Nor were the sailing performances of the French-built ships one whit behind the promise suggested by their good looks.

"Madeleine," "Caroline" and "Montmorency."

A. D. Bordes' first order for bounty ships went to the Ateliers et Chantiers de la Loire at Nantes for the three steel sister four-mast barques *Madeleine*, *Caroline* and *Montmorency*.

The registered dimensions of these ships were as follows:—Length 322 ft. 1 in.; breadth 45 ft.; depth 25 ft. 5 ins.; gross tons 3011, net 2376. *Madeleine* was launched in January 1896, *Caroline* in May and *Montmorency* in June.

Of the three ships, *Caroline*, after making some good passages such as:

1897	Caleta Buena to Prawle Point	74 days
1900-1	Iquique to Dunkirk	74 „
1901	Scilly to Iquique	81 „

was lost on her next passage.

Madeleine must have had very nearly the best record of all Bordes' ships, her chief sailing performances being as follows:

1896 Left Iquique June 18. Arrived Lizard August 26, 69 days

1897 Left Shields April 19. Arrived Valparaiso July 4. 73 days from Prawle Point

1897-8 Left Shields November 19, 1897. Arrived Valparaiso January 25, 1898. 66 days

1898 Left Iquique February 19. Arrived Lizard May 10. 79 days.

On her outward passage in 1899 the *Madeleine* had a great race with her sister ship *Montmorency* and the *A. D. Bordes*, all three vessels arriving in Valparaiso Bay on May 1.

A. D. Bordes was the winner of the race. She left Shields on February 18, passed Dover on the 20th and was only 70 days from that point; the *Madeleine* was 71 days from the Downs, and *Montmorency* 72 days from Prawle Point.

The two sister ships, *Madeleine* and *Montmorency* had another great contest on the homeward passage. After a ding-dong struggle *Madeleine* arrived off Dungeness on August 7, 1899, 81 days out from Iquique, and on the same day *Montmorency* made her number off the Lizard.

In 1901 *Madeleine* made the nitrate passage in 85 days, arriving Gravelines on July 5.

In 1902 she again made a fine outward run. Leaving Shields on May 5, she passed the Lizard on May 8, and arrived Iquique on July 17, just 70 days from the Lizard.

Her last passage of any note was made in 1903, when she ran from Iquique to the Lizard in 78 days.

A ship's reputation is in the hands of her captain, and a vessel which has a fine sailing record and then suddenly drops out of the list of good passage makers will generally be found to have changed a passage-making captain for one who is not a sail carrier, or in Cape Horn voyages for one who snugged down to lower topsails directly he got in the latitude of Cape Stiff and trusted to a slant to take his vessel round the corner instead of acting on the wise advice of "Make westing, drive her and make westing."

Montmorency never beat her outward passage in the 1879 race. Her next best was Barry to Iquique, 73 days in 1902, when she came home to Dungeness in 84 days.

Her passages in 1903 were 79 days out from the Isle of Wight to Iquique and the same number of days home from Iquique to Dover.

In 1903-4, however, she made a very smart passage home. Leaving Iquique November 12, 1903, she arrived Hamburg on January 24, 1904, only 73 days out.

Montmorency survived to the end of Bordes et Fils' career as sailing ship owners, being sold in 1926.

"JEANNE D'ARC"

Lent by Captain L. R. W. Beavis

[*See page* 139

OLD TEA CLIPPER "LOTHAIR"
On the West Coast

Lent by Captain L. R. W. Beavis. Photo by H. H. Morrison [*See page* 143

"Wulfrun Puget" and "Perseverance."

Two other sister ships were built for A. D. Bordes in 1896. These were the *Wulfrun Puget* and *Perseverance*, constructed at La Seyne by the Forges et Chantiers de la Mediterranee.

The measurements and tonnage were as follows:—Length 322 ft. 2 ins.; breadth 45 ft. 7 ins.; depth 25 ft. 4 ins.; tons gross 2990, net 2415. Their poops were 49 ft. long, foc's'le 53 feet, and the break 11 feet. The *Wulfrun Puget* was launched in April, 1896, and the *Perseverance* in August. It will be noticed that their superstructure was slightly less than the Nantes-built three, whilst they had a foot more of length and 7 inches more of beam.

In sailing capabilities there was very little to choose; in fact, this was the case with all Bordes' bounty-built four-mast barques their records simply depending on their captains, and a crack passage maker could get the same results from any one of them.

Wulfrun Puget's best voyage was made in 1903, under Captain L. Quenet. On February 23 she arrived at Iquique, 73 days from Dungeness, and on her nitrate passage she passed the Isle of Wight on June 2, 74 days out from Iquique. Though she equalled these passages on more than one occasion, she never surpassed them. The *Perseverance*, which by the way was the third ship of that name, made a 71-day passage from Portland to Valparaiso in 1898. Her best nitrate passage was 74 days made the previous year.

Wulfrun Puget survived until 1926, but the *Perseverance* was put under by a German submarine in 1917.

"Rhone," "Antoinette" and "Jacqueline."

These three sister ships were also built at La Seyne, the *Rhone* being launched October, 1896, *Antoinette* in February, 1897, and *Jacqueline* in June, 1897.

Their measurements were the same as the previous pair, but their tonnage came out as follows:—Gross 3017, net 2434.

Antoinette seems to have had the best record with the following good passages:

1897	Iquique to Dungeness	..	78 days
1900	Isle of Wight to Iquique	..	72 „
1901	Iquique to Dunkirk	..	84 „
1902	Iquique to Isle of Wight	..	81 „
1902	Iquique to Dungeness	..	84 „
1905	Iquique to Dungeness	..	72 „
1906	Shields to Iquique	..	76 „
1906	La Pallice to Mejillones	..	74 „

Rhone's best outward passage was one of 73 days from Beachy Head to Iquique in 1902, and her best homeward, Iquique to Lizard, 78 days in 1902. *Jacqueline's* best outward was from Barry to Iquique 72 days in 1906, and the best homeward that I can find is Iquique to Dunkirk, 86 days in 1901.

A very curious accident happened to the *Jacqueline* in August, 1907. When in tow of a tug she came into collision with a Cornish headland, when her chief damage was the crumpling up of her steel bowsprit. On August 21 she was dry-docked and repaired at Falmouth.

This beautiful ship was sunk by a German submarine in 1917. *Antoinette* was lost in 1918, but the *Rhone* survived until 1926, when she was disposed of.

The "Dunkerque."

This ship, which I have already mentioned as an example of the type produced by the French Navigation Bounty Laws, seems to have been built as an experiment, for, contrary to custom, she was not followed by the usual sister ships from the same yard.

Yet, as the following records testify, she was one of the most successful passage makers in the nitrate fleet:

1897	Left	Iquique,	June	15	Arrived	off Lizard,	Aug.	24	70 days
1897	,,	Dungeness,	Sept.	25	,,	Valparaiso,	Dec.	3	69 ,,
1898	,,	Caleta Buena,	Aug.	13	,,	off Lizard,	Oct.	31	79 ,,
1899	,,	Iquique,	March	17	,,	off Scilly,	June	5	80 ,,
1899	,,	Bishop,	July	10	,,	Valparaiso,	Sept.	17	69 ,,
1899-1900	,,	Iquique,	Oct.	21	,,	Prawle Pt.,	Jan.	7,1900	78 ,,
1900	,,	,,	May	5	,,	,,	July	24	80 ,,
1902	,,	,,	March	25	,,	Isle of Wight,	June	13	82 ,,
1903	,,	,,	June	23	,,	Prawle Pt.,	Sept.	2	72 ,,
1905	,,	Port Talbot,	Oct.	17	,,	Iquique,	Dec.	23	67 ,,
1909-10	,,	Iquique,	Nov.	16	,,	Antwerp,	Jan.	31 1910	76 ,,
1912	,,	Talcahuano,	Sept.	14	,,	Dunkirk,	Dec.	10	87 ,,

This fine ship was sold in 1924.

"Loire" and "Atlantique."

This pair came from the slips of the Loire shipbuilders at Nantes, the *Loire* in March, 1897, and the *Atlantique* in June of the same year.

The difference between them and the first three was very slight; measurements of the hull and superstructure were the same, only the tonnage was bigger, being 3094 tons gross and 2453 net. Both ships had excellent sailing records, of which the following are the best:

"LOIRE."

1897	Left	Portland,	April 18	Arrived	Iquique,	June 23	66	days
1898	„	Beachy Head,	Dec. 1	„	Valparaiso,	Feb. 9	69	„
1898	„	Iquique,	March 5	„	Prawle Pt.,	May 19	75	„
1898	„	„	Sept. 18	„	Gravelines,	Dec. 6	79	„
1900	„	Dunkirk,	March 15	„	Iquique,	May 29	75	„
1900	„	Antwerp,	Oct. 7	„	Iquique,	Dec. 18	72	„
1901	„	Iquique,	Jan. 1	„	Prawle Pt.,	March 27	86	„
1901	„	„	Sept. 6	„	Isle of Wight,	Dec. 1	86	„
1903	„	„	Dec. 16	„	Off Lizard,	March 6	80	„

"ATLANTIQUE."

1899	Left	Caleta Buena,	Feb. 23	Arrived	Prawle Pt.,	May 12	78	days
1902	„	Iquique,	Aug. 23	„	Isle of Wight,	Oct. 22	75	„
1902-3	„	Lizard,	Dec. 3	„	Iquique,	Feb. 17	76	„
1905	„	Port Talbot,	Jan. 20	„	„	March 28	67	„
1905	„	„	Aug. 28	„	„	Nov. 7	71	„
1907	„	Iquique,	April 7	„	Dunkirk,	June 17	71	„
1916	„	La Pallice,	Oct. 3	„	Mejillones,	Dec. 16	74	„

The *Loire* was sold in 1924 and the *Atlantique* in 1926.

Bordes Buys Two of Lyle's "Capes."

In 1899 the two sister ships, *Cape Clear* and *Cape York*, of 2129 tons gross, were bought at the dispersal of Lyle's sugar fleet. These fine steel four-mast barques, the first of which was built by Duncan and the second by Barclay Curle, had a very short career in the nitrate trade, for the *Cape Clear* went missing in 1900 and the *Cape York* was lost in 1905.

Messrs. Bordes' other addition to their fleet in 1899 was equally unlucky. This was a big three-mast barque called *Seine*, built by La Porte at Rouen. She was an extreme example of the bounty type. Her gross tonnage was 2630, whilst her net was only 1587, over 1000 tons difference. In her rig she was tremendously square without any depth to her topsails and topgallant sails.

I remember seeing several of these bounty-built three-mast barques lying in Table Bay waiting to discharge in 1901-2 during the South African War. They were extremely handsome as regards looks, and with poop and topgallant foc's'le almost meeting they looked higher out of the water and therefore more seaworthy than the Britishers anchored near them. And they were successful, from the financial point of view, so that a great number of them were built in French yards.

The *Seine*, however, did not last long being lost in 1900.

"Marthe" and "Valentine."

With the advent of the new century A. D. Bordes launched out with the magnificent sister four-mast barques, *Marthe* and *Valentine*, built at Grand Quevilly by the Chantiers de Normandie. *Marthe* was sent off the stocks in December, 1900, and the *Valentine* in April, 1901. Again we find the difference between gross and net tonnage, *Marthe* registering 3119 and 2432, and *Valentine* a ton more. This difference was accounted for by poops of 72 feet, foc's'les of 86 feet and the usual 10 ft. break.

Messrs. A. D. Bordes consider that the *Valentine* made the finest outward passage round the Horn ever put up by any of their fleet. She left Shields on November 24, 1903, and arrived at Iquique on January 29, 1904, a run of 66 days from port to port.

But she only just beat her sister ship which sailed from Port Talbot on November 19, 1903, and anchored in Iquique on January 28, 1904, the day before the *Valentine*, her passage being 70 days. This is the only passage of note that I can find under *Marthe's* name, but the *Valentine* made an equally fine run this voyage with her homeward cargo of nitrate.

Leaving Iquique on February 25, 1904, she reached Dunkirk on May 5, just 70 days out. L. Gardanne was her captain. He took her from the stocks, and in 1902 he had also made the best passage home of the Bordes' fleet. He left Iquique on April 13, and arrived at Falmouth on June 25, 73 days out.

Other good passages made by this ship were:

1901	Iquique to the Lizard	..	85 days
1903	Lizard to Valparaiso	..	76 „
1912	Port Talbot to Iquique	..	87 „
1912	Iquique to Dunkirk	..	79 „

Both *Marthe* and *Valentine* fell victims to the war, the *Valentine* being caught and sunk by a German cruiser in 1914 and the *Marthe* by a submarine in 1917.

"Adolphe" and "Alexandre."

Bordes' next pair of four-mast barques, the *Adolphe* and *Alexandre*, were launched at Dunkirk in 1902. These were big ships with a net tonnage of 2462 and a cargo capacity of 3910 tons, reckoning the ton at 1000 kilos. One cannot say much about them, however, as the *Alexandre* was lost in 1903 and the *Adolphe* in 1904.

"Rancagua," "Quillota" and "Madeleine (2).

Like many other sailing ship owners, Messrs. A. D. Bordes fell to the temptation of the big three-master, and in 1902 the St. Nazaire shipbuilders launched the steel full-rigged ships *Rancagua* and *Madeleine* (2) and the three-mast barque *Quillota* to the order of the great nitrate firm.

As regards dimensions and superstructures these three ships

were sisters with a length of 282 ft. 8 ins.; beam of 44 ft. 1 in.; and depth of 22 ft. 7 ins. They were built to take full advantage of the bounty with practically a hurricane deck over the main-deck, their poops measuring 136 feet long, topgallant foc's'les 49 feet and midship bridges of 44 feet.

In tonnage there were some slight differences, as follows:

	Gross	Net
Rancagua	2719	2315
Madeleine (2) ..	2852	1875
Quillota	2559	2073

Not since the days of the wooden Black Ball and White Star clippers have big three-masters made a success of sail propulsion, and these big Frenchmen were no exception to the rule. Here are three average passages made in 1912-1913:

Rancagua	Tyne to Iquique	Arrived	Oct.	20, 1912	118 days
Quillota	Iquique to Bruges	„	Feb.	8, 1913	113 days
Madeleine (2)	Tyne to Iquique	„	Feb.	8, 1913	94 „

All three vessels fell victims to the war in 1917.

"Reine Blanche," "Amiral Troude" and "Brenn."

In 1896-7 La Porte of Rouen built two steel three-mast barques for Raoul Guillon of Nantes, the *Reine Blanche* and *Amiral Troude*; whilst in 1900 the St. Nazaire builders sent the steel three-mast barque *Brenn* afloat to the order of the Celtique Maritime of Nantes. These three were not such extreme bounty ships as the *Rancagua*, *Madeleine* and *Quillota*, their dimensions being:

	Tons gross	Tons net	Length	Breadth	Depth
Reine Blanche	1854	1653	263·3	36·7	21·4
Amiral Troude	1949	1417	263·8	36·7	21·4
Brenn ..	2300	1707	279·1	40·2	22·7

The first two came under Bordes' house-flag soon after

the turn of the century, but *Brenn* only a short while before the war. None of the three made any outstanding sailing records that I know of; indeed they could not compete with Bordes' beautiful four-masters.

Both *Brenn* and *Amiral Troude* were sunk by German submarines in 1917, but the *Reine Blanche* survived to be sold in 1923.

"Antonin" and "Valparaiso."

The last two sailing ships to be specially built for A. D. Bordes et Fils were the big four-mast barques *Antonin* and *Valparaiso*, which were launched at Dunkirk, the former in September and the latter in November of 1902.

They were sister ships with the following measurements:

	Tons gross	Tons net	Length	Beam	Depth
Antonin ..	3071	2662	313·5	45	24·2
Valparaiso ..	3081	2664	313·6	45·1	24·3

They did not have so much superstructure as the three-masters, their poops being 72 ft. long and foc's'le-heads 88 feet.

They soon showed that they could sail in company with any of Bordes' previous ships. In 1903 *Valparaiso* came home from Iquique to Prawle Point in 80 days; and in 1904 *Antonin* left Port Talbot on October 1, and reached Iquique on December 15, 75 days out. She beat this fine outward passage round the Horn during the height of the war. Leaving La Pallice on November 18, 1915, she arrived at Antofagasta on January 29, 1916, only 72 days out. She was sunk by the German cruiser *Seeadler* the following year.

Valparaiso was luckier and was not sold until 1927.

"PAMIR" IN THE ICE AT ROTTERDAM, 1929

Lent by E. W. Petrejus. [*See page* 149.

Bordes et Fils buy some Noted British Ships.

Between 1905 and 1910 the great French nitrate firm bought no less than nine well-known British windjammers. These were:

Peleus and *Glaucus*, from Carmichael's Golden Fleece Line.

Strathdon, from the Aberdeen White Star Line.

Springburn, from Shankland's Burn Line.

Burmah, from Foley & Co., of London.

Achnashie, from Thom & Cameron, for which they paid £10,500 in 1907 or at the rate of £4 9s. per ton.

Muskoka, that famous modern clipper, which, sailed by her noted Blue-nose skipper, Albert Crowe, had the finest record of modern times as a passage maker and was considered by many shipping people to be the fastest steel sailing ship ever built.

Andorinha, which had the honour of being the biggest ship in the fleet during the time that she flew Bordes' house-flag.

Marion Josiah, a big Connell-built four-mast barque from Rogers' Marion Line.

All these Britishers were disguised under the usual A. D. Bordes names. The *Peleus*, bought in 1905, became the fourth *Adolphe*. This beautiful full rigger, the last of the superb Carmichael fleet, survived the war to be broken up at Dordrecht in October, 1923.

Glaucus, which in 1909 made a run of 76 days between Shields and Valparaiso under her new name of *Almendral*, was also sold by Bordes in 1923.

This likewise was the fate of *Strathdon*, which had become the third *Gers*. It will be remembered that this handsome barque was sent afloat by Harland & Wolff under the name of *Queen's Island*.

The bald-header *Springburn* became the *Alexandre*; *Burmah* was renamed *Coquimbo* and *Achnashie* became *Chanaral*, whilst *Marion Josiah* was given the favourite Bordes name of *Tijuca*. Every one of these four ships succumbed to that terrible engine of war, the German submarine.

Muskoka was renamed *Caroline*.

The following are her most noteworthy passages under the French flag:

1912	Iquique to La Pallice: 91 days
1912-3	Port Talbot to Iquique: 87 days
1916	Nantes to Taltal, February 21 to April 30: 69 days
1916	St. Nazaire to Antofagasta October 16 to December 25: 70 days

In July, 1920, the sad news came over the wires that this famous ship had been burnt out and beached at Antofagasta.

The big *Andorinha* was renamed *Helene*. She also survived the war but was lost in 1919.

Last Purchases by Bordes.

The following is a list of Bordes' last purchases:

General Neumayer, steel three-mast barque, built by La Porte at Rouen in 1897 for N. Guillon, 1858 tons gross; 1640 tons net; length 263.3; beam 36 ft. 7 ins.; depth 21 ft. 4 ins. Sold out of the Bordes fleet in 1923.

Cambronne, steel three-mast barque, built by La Porte on same lines and same year as *General Neumayer* for the Society Anonyme des Voilers, Nantes. She was captured by Von Luckner of *Seeadler* fame, and sent into Rio under Captain Mullings, with 287 prisoners.

Europe and *Asie*, four-mast barques of 2839 tons gross, also built by La Porte in 1897. These two were first of all the property of A. D'Orbigny, Faustin & Co., of La Rochelle.

The *Europe* was another submarine victim in that fatal year of 1917 and *Asie* was lost in 1919.

One of Bordes' last purchases was the steel three-mast barque *Belen* of 2202 tons, which was renamed *Jeanne d'Arc.* This ship was built on the Loire in 1901 for the Societe Navale de l'Oceanie, was sold to the Celtique Maritime of Nantes and then to A. D. Bordes et Fils. She was sold out of the Bordes fleet in 1923.

The last two ships to come under Bordes' house-flag were the big four-mast barques *Emilie Siegfried* and *Ernest Siegfried,* which were built by the Forges et Chantiers de la Mediterranean at Havre in 1898-9 for Ed. Corblet & Co., of Havre.

These big sister ships registered 3104 tons gross and 2754 net; length 312 ft.; beam 45 ft. 4 ins.; depth 24 ft. 6 ins. Like all bounty-built ships they had much superstructure, their poops being 115 ft. long and topgallant foc's'les 86 feet.

In 1911 they were bought by the Societe Navale de l'Oceanie and renamed *Sainte Marguerite* and *Sainte Catherine.* Then just before the outbreak of war they were acquired by A. D. Bordes et Fils, and renamed *Blanche* and *Seine.*

Blanche was torpedoed in 1917 and *Seine* sold in 1923.

It is sad to think that this famous fleet of sailing ships is now no more, and that some half-dozen steamers alone represent the Bordes firm upon the high seas. Even the old name is concealed under the usual lengthy French title of Compagnie Francaise d'Armement et d'Importation de Nitrate de Soude.

The Progress of Ant. Dom. Bordes et Fils.

Statistics showing the steady rise of this great firm are interesting as a comparison with those of noted British firms.

Indeed, I think British shipowners might find some difficulty in matching the Bordes record.

In 1870 the firm possessed 15 sailing ships, carrying 16,830 tons of 1000 kilos.

Five years later and the Bordes fleet had increased to 34 ships capable of loading 39,335 tons.

In 1880 there were 40 ships with an effective cargo capacity of 45,765 tons. In 1885 the fleet was only one ship stronger, but the tonnage had risen to 51,975; and by 1890 the number of ships had dropped to 31, but with a big increase in the size of each ship, giving a carriage power of 62,550 tons.

In 1895 with the same number of ships the cargo capacity had again risen over 10,000 tons to 73,930; and by 1900, at which date British owners were beginning to sell their ships at scrap prices, the Bordes fleet had a total of 38 ships carrying 119,560 tons. By 1905 the fleet had dropped 3 ships, but again the tonnage was up—to 123,070 tons. Five years later there were 42 ships capable of 150,100 tons of cargo under the Bordes flag. And in 1914 when war broke out, Ant. Dom. Bordes et Fils were at the height of their prosperity with a fleet of 46 ships capable of transporting 163,160 tons.

Of course, it may be argued, that the French Bounty Laws may have had a great deal to do with the firm's success; but Messrs. A. D. Bordes et Fils themselves have some justification for their contention that it was business acumen and foresight, good management and well run ships of good construction which contributed 90 per cent. to their success, leaving 10 per cent., let us say, for the bounty and other lesser factors.

A. D. Bordes and F. Laeisz Compared to British Owners.

I have been at some pains to give a full description of the two splendid fleets of nitrate ships, owned respectively by A. D. Bordes et Fils and F. Laeisz as being worthy to be compared with the very best of our sailing ship lines at the height of our shipping prosperity.

Indeed there is no doubt that our sailing ship managers could have learnt a great deal from these two foreign firms, the one French and the other German.

In fact, one must confess that they pretty well succeeded in ousting British ships from one of their most paying trades. Indeed by 1914 British ships were clean out of the running in the West Coast trade. I should not like to say whether A. D. Bordes or F. Laeisz came first, but have little hesitation in asserting that it was a case of the rest nowhere, with regard to their rivals on the West Coast, whether they were British or any other nationality.

If statistics could be compiled showing how much Welsh and Tyne coal was carried round the Horn to the Chilean ports by Bordes ships from first to last, I think it would somewhat astonish the British free trader. Indeed I think Messrs. A. D. Bordes would be the first to acknowledge that their success in business would not have been so spectacular if the ports of Cardiff, Port Talbot and the Tyne had been closed to them.

Cross Pacific Statistics.

The ships of Bordes and Laeisz nearly always loaded outward direct to the West Coast by way of Cape Horn.

But right up to the outbreak of war in 1914 there was a big sailing ship fleet of all nationalities carrying coal across the

Pacific from Newcastle, N.S.W., to the nitrate ports of Chile. This was one of the last strongholds of British sail.

British sailing ship owners had had the mortification of seeing themselves ousted from the Calcutta jute trade, the Australian wheat trade, the Californian grain trade and even the lumber trade; and at the present day not a single British sailing ship remains even to take a share in the annual race home round the Horn with Australian wheat.

But in 1914 the Pacific traverse still could show that British sail was not entirely dead.

Let us take some statistics from Lloyd's Shipping Index. I have before me the year 1912. For the last six months of 1912 I find that 106 sailing ships sailed from Newcastle, N.S.W., to West Coast ports.

This fine fleet consisted of:

39 ships under the Red Ensign.
23 ships under German colours (11 of which were *ex* Britishers).
20 Norwegian ships (15 of which were *ex* Britishers).
10 French ships.
6 Russian ships (5 of which were *ex* Britishers).
5 Italian ships (3 of which were *ex* Britishers).
2 Swedish ships (1 of which was an *ex* Britisher).
1 Danish ship.

The best passage was made by the German ship, *Suzanne Vinnen,* which sailing from Newcastle, N.S.W., on October 4 arrived at Talcahuano on November 6, 33 days out.

Next to her came another German ship the *Edmund,* ex *William Tell,* which arrived at Valparaiso on October 30, 34 days out from Newcastle. Then came the old Aberdeen clipper *Pericles,* sailing under Norwegian colours, which arrived at Valparaiso on October 19, 39 days out.

North Pacific to South Pacific Passages.

Up to the outbreak of war in August, 1914, there was a flourishing lumber trade from North Pacific to South Pacific ports, but few of the vessels in this trade loaded nitrate home.

Taking the same period as that of the Pacific coal records just given, I find that between June, 1912, and January 1913, there were no less than 52 American sailing ships carrying lumber South, 3 Chilean, 2 Peruvian and 1 Italian and 1 German.

The Americans were all wood four-mast schooners and barquentines with the exception of the old wood ship *William H. Smith* and two great five-mast schooners the *Luca* and *W. H. Marston.*

The Chilean ships consisted of the old British iron barque *Royal Sovereign,* the *Curzon*—which began life as a steamer in 1865—and the lordly four-mast ship, *County of Linlithgow,* the last of Craig's "Counties."

The Peruvians were both old British ships, the *Cockermouth* and *Lothair.* The latter, which was none other than the famous tea clipper, built by Walker on the Thames in 1870, had long been a familiar sight on the West Coast, belonging to the port of Callao and sailing under the flag of F. G. Piaggio.

The photograph, though it shows her in ballast and under barque rig, gives one a very good hint of what this little composite thoroughbred must have looked like in her racing days. It is easy for the nautical eye to take in the fineness of her lines and the shapeliness of her ends. She was of the same delicate beauty as *Ariel, Titania* and *Sir Lancelot,* and she was considered to be quite as speedy as any of these famous three.

Lothair survived the war, and I believe is still afloat.

The Italian timber ship was named *Cavour*. This was none other than the old *Commonwealth*, the ship in which I fell from aloft, just on thirty years ago. She also came under the Peruvian flag, and under the name of *Cuatro Hermanos* was owned in Callao at the end of the war.

It seems only recently that British shipping papers were printing columns and showing photographs of her dignified end. It will be remembered that she quietly sank at her moorings at Antofagasta in 1927, being then named *Sofia*.

Though I am doubtful whether the little *Lothair* ever raced home with a nitrate cargo, the *Commonwealth* hoisted an excited apprentice aloft on her last bag of nitrate on a good many occasions. I should like to be able to say that she had beaten the *Potosi* or the *France* on the run home round the Horn, but I am afraid I can find no evidence of such a glorious victory.

A Lamentable Fact.

Alas! that the good old West Coast days have passed! When the *William Mitchell*, the last square-rigged windjammer belonging to the port of London, loaded a nitrate cargo at Tocopilla in August, 1927, on what proved to be her last voyage, there was not another sailing ship in the anchorage.

And when her crew, keen as mustard to keep up all the old customs of the sea, went through the ceremony of cheering ship as the last bag was hoisted aboard, not one of the dingy steamers lying around her even took the trouble to ring her bell!

How are the mighty fallen!

In the days of sail the sea was a great commonwealth. Sailors whatever their colour, whatever their nationality, were all dipped in the same tar bucket, ground in the same mould, and tested and proved by those three mighty character makers, wind, sea and canvas.

They were loyal to their ships because they loved them; and they were artists in their profession, that great profession of sailorising which is now almost defunct.

Seafaring is now given over to deck sweepers and brass polishers—to men with sweat rags round their necks—to men in overall suits of dungaree, whose hands, ingrained with oil and coal-dust, would make a sad hash of stowing a topsail in a gale of wind.

And what do they think of British seamen on the West Coast in these troublous days?

No wonder that so many are agitating for sail training once more under the Red Ensign.

Even as I write, the news comes in that the *Peking* has arrived at Talcahuano (August 15, 1931) only 73 days out from Hamburg. That time, outward round the Horn, spells "fine ships, fine sailormen."

At the present moment, where such ship handling and sailorizing are concerned, Great Britain is a "has-been."

Possibly it is better than being a "never was'er"—but not much!

Adios.

APPENDIX

APPENDIX

INDEX

INDEX

INDEX

INDEX

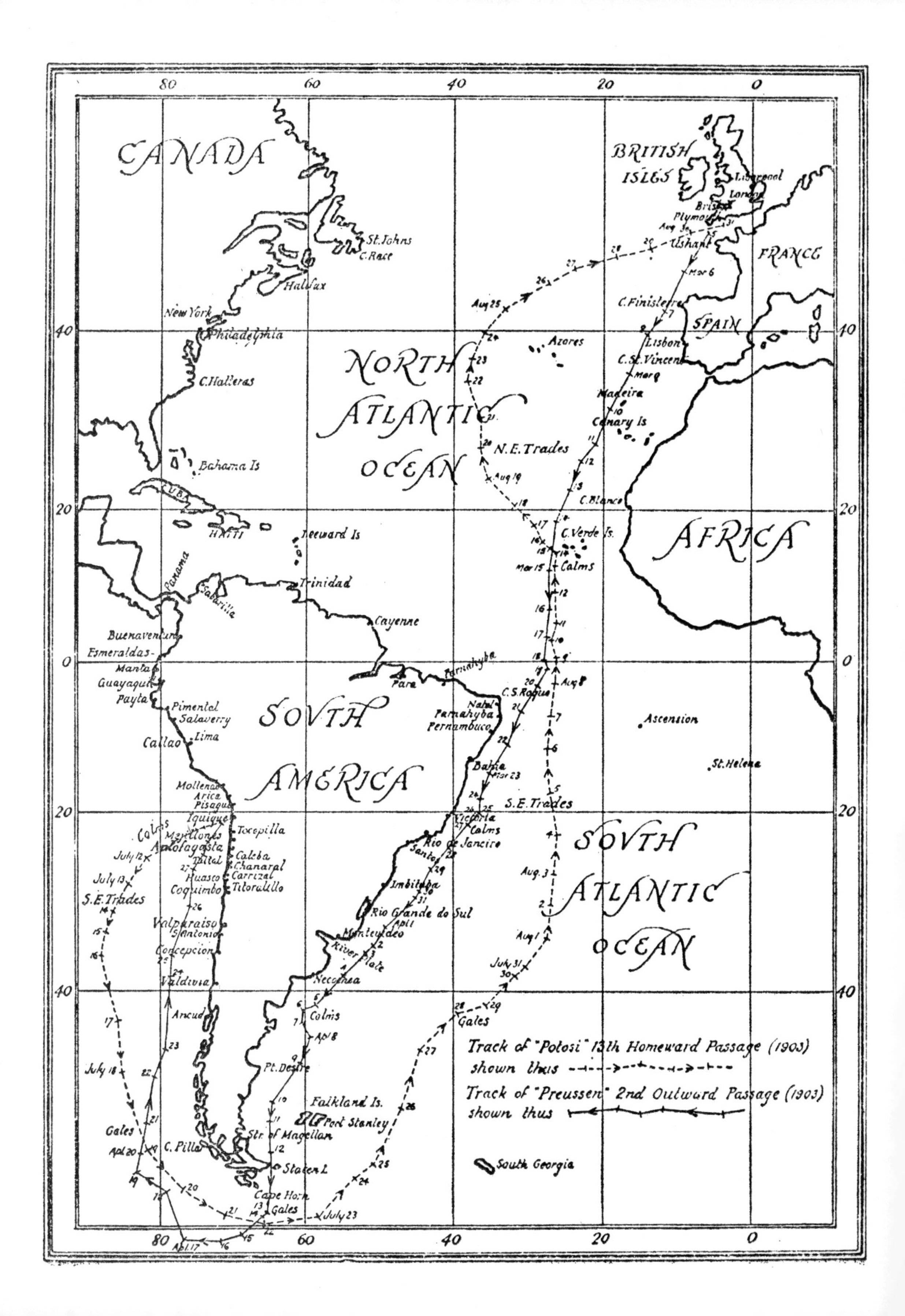
CANADA
BRITISH ISLES
Liverpool
London
Bristol
Plymouth
Ushant
FRANCE
SPAIN
Lisbon
C. St. Vincent
C. Finisterre
Madeira
Canary Is
Azores
St. Johns
C. Race
Halifax
New York
Philadelphia
C. Hatteras
Bahama Is
HAITI
Leeward Is
Trinidad
Cayenne
Panama
Sabanilla
NORTH ATLANTIC OCEAN
N. E. Trades
C. Blanco
C. Verde Is.
Calms
AFRICA
Ascension
St. Helena
SOUTH AMERICA
Buenaventura
Esmeraldas
Manta
Guayaquil
Payta
Pimentel
Salaverry
Callao
Lima
Mollendo
Arica
Pisagua
Iquique
Tocopilla
Mejillones
Antofagasta
Taltal
Caleta
Chanaral
Carrizal
Huasco
Coquimbo
Totoralillo
Valparaiso
S. Antonio
Concepcion
Valdivia
Ancud
C. Pillar
Para
Parnahyba
Natal
Pernambuco
C. S. Roque
Bahia
Victoria
Rio de Janeiro
Santos
Imbituba
Rio Grande do Sul
Montevideo
River Plate
Necochea
Colms
Pt. Desire
Falkland Is.
Port Stanley
Str. of Magellan
Staten I.
Cape Horn
Gales
S. E. Trades
SOUTH ATLANTIC OCEAN
South Georgia
Track of "Potosi" 13th Homeward Passage (1903) shown thus
Track of "Preussen" 2nd Outward Passage (1903) shown thus